Land Sea & Sky

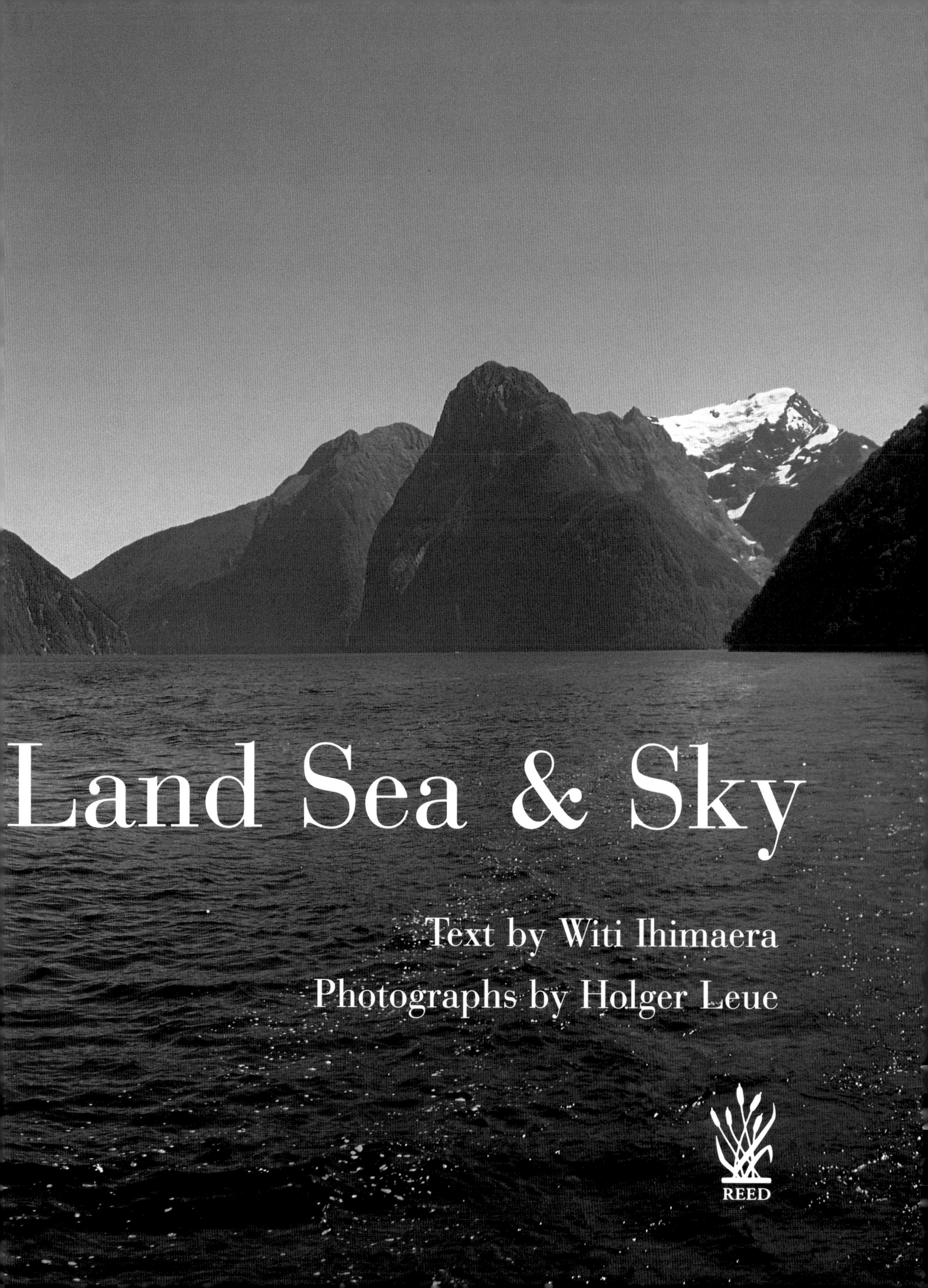

Land Sea & Sky

Text by Witi Ihimaera
Photographs by Holger Leue

Also by Holger Leue:

Epiphyllum — The Splendor of Leaf Cacti (1987)
The Legendary Land (1994)

Also by Witi Ihimaera:

Pounamu, Pounamu (1972)
Tangi (1973)
Whanau (1974)
The New Net Goes Fishing (1977)
Into the World of Light (ed. with D.S. Long, 1982)
The Matriarch (1986)
The Whale Rider (1987)
Dear Miss Mansfield (1989)
Te Ao Marama (ed., 5 volumes, 1992–)
Bulibasha (1994)
The Legendary Land (1994)

First published in 1994 by Reed Books, a division of Reed Publishing (NZ) Ltd, 39 Rawene Road, Birkenhead, Auckland. Associated companies, branches and representatives throughout the world.

This book is copyright. Except for the purpose of fair reviewing, no part of this publication may be reproduced or transmitted in any form or by any means, electronic or mechanical, including photocopying, recording, or any information storage and retrieval system, without permission in writing from the publisher. Infringers of copyright render themselves liable to prosecution.

© 1994 Reed Publishing

ISBN 0 7900 0379 1 modern
ISBN 0 7900 0380 5 traditional

Cover and text design by Chris Lipscombe.
Printed by Everbest Printing Co, Hong Kong.

Previous page: Milford Sound, Fiordland.

Contents

Te Reinga to Auckland   6

Waikato to the Volcanic Plateau   26

Coromandel to the Wairarapa   46

Taranaki to Wellington   64

Marlborough and Nelson to Kaikoura   76

Christchurch and Canterbury   88

The West Coast   104

Dunedin and Otago   120

Murihiku: The South   138

Acknowledgements   160

The gateway to Auckland's Aotea Centre, the work of Maori artist Selwyn Muru.

Te Reinga to Auckland

Tradition has it that Northland is where Kupe, the Maori discoverer of Aotearoa, landed. When he took the news back to the legendary Hawaiki it was of a place of sunshine, beauty and incredible potential. The east coast is a complex of deep harbours with names that roll off the tongue like breakers coming in from the sea — Parengarenga, Houhora, Kerikeri — down to Whangarei, the main city of the north. The west coast is a maze of estuaries and shallow harbours, dominated by the Hokianga Harbour. Everywhere there are long sandy beaches and small sun-baked settlements snoozing in the sun.

Once upon a time the rugged hills were totally covered with the kauri, King of Trees; although the majority were felled for the early shipbuilding industry there are still some stands remaining to remind us of the imposing forests that touched the sky. Other places are haunted with memories of the kauri gumlands, where Maori and Dalmatian worked together.

The Bay of Islands was the cradle of both Maori and Pakeha settlement and it was here that the Treaty of Waitangi was signed in 1840. From the grounds of the Treaty House you can look across to Paihia and Russell. Nearby Okiato was the site of New Zealand's first capital, although this was soon moved to Auckland.

Sprawled across the isthmus between the Manukau and Waitemata Harbours, Auckland has grown from a shantytown on the beach to become New Zealand's largest city, and the largest Polynesian city in the world.

Today Auckland is in fact four cities — Auckland City itself, North Shore City, Manukau City and Waitakere City. The centrepiece of Auckland City is Queen Street, which runs up from the harbour to Karangahape Road, but throughout there are suburbs of distinctive charm and individuality. The dance clubs and restaurants of Ponsonby, Herne Bay, Parnell, Mission Bay and Devonport are always busy, while the Polynesian markets of South Auckland are vibrant and alive.

Auckland's natural configuration is complicated by volcanic cones, the most dramatic of which is Rangitoto Island. More than any other feature, Rangitoto is a physical icon for Aucklanders, symbolising their love of the outdoors and their wonderful harbour.

Native flax provides a graphic foreground to the Hokianga Harbour, on Northland's west coast.

Kerikeri was the second Anglican mission station in Aotearoa New Zealand, and the Stone Store is the oldest surviving stone building in the country. Nearby are the beautiful Rainbow Falls. Orchards abound near Kerikeri, the country's premier citrus-growing area.

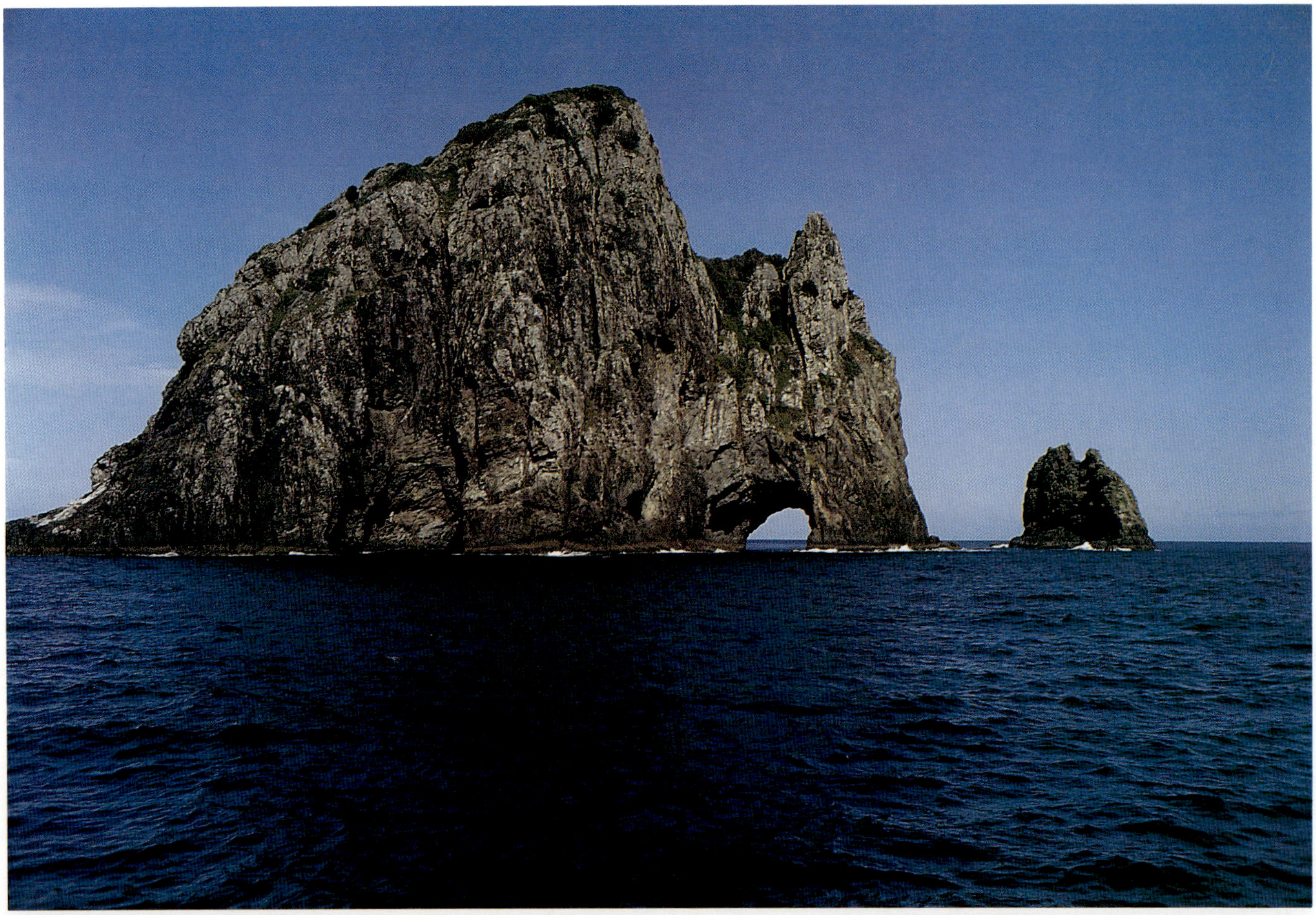

Fullers
TOKERAU
Fullers

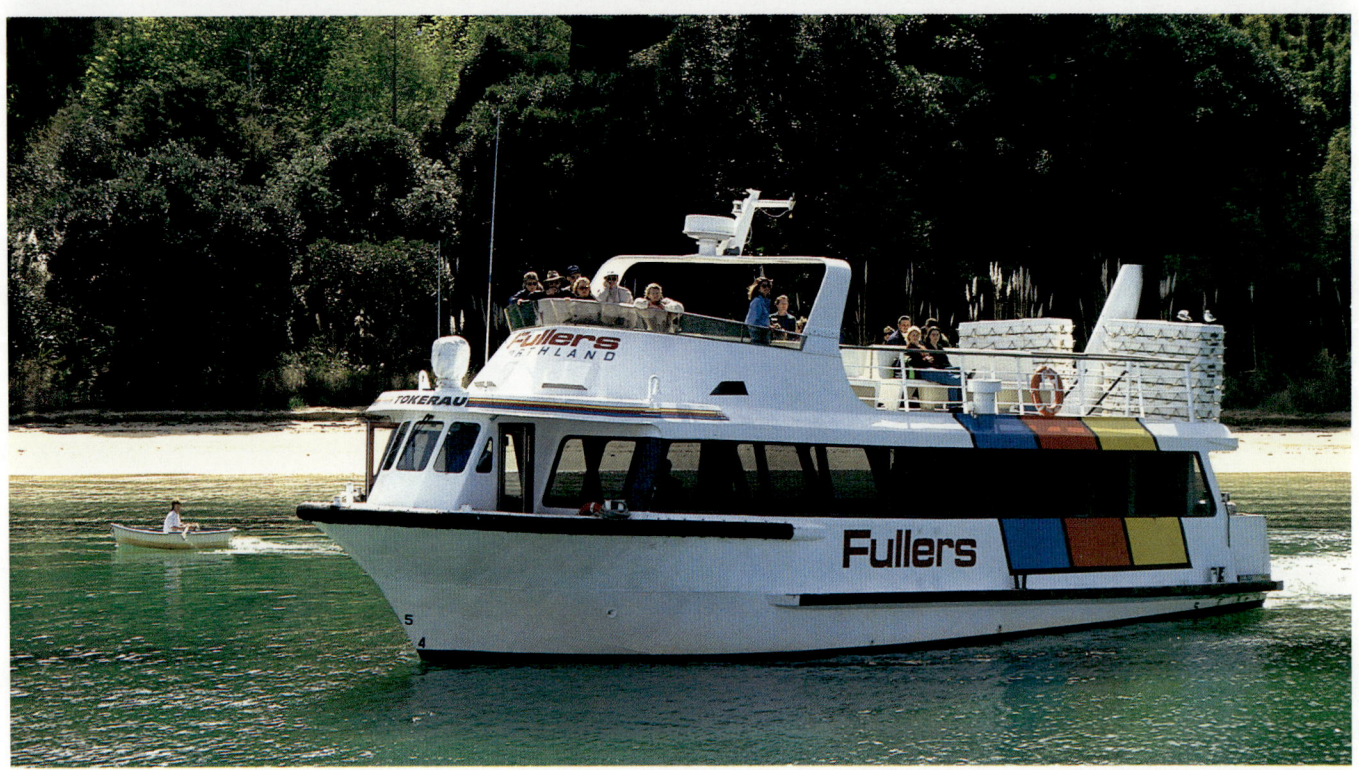

Once a haven for tall whaling ships, the Bay of Islands is still a favourite destination of sailors, sunseekers and fishers. Cruises include the Fullers Mailboat, which delivers mail to the more isolated bays of the coast, and the fascinating Hole in the Rock. Later on, where better to relax than Russell's historic Duke of Marlborough Hotel?

The sundial on Russell's Flagstaff Hill overlooks the town and the superb Bay of Islands.

Pompallier House, which stands on Russell's waterfront, is now a museum illustrating the early days of Russell and the French mission which was based here under Bishop Pompallier. Traditional printing crafts are now undertaken here, recreating the mission's major activity last century.

The seagoing waka, or canoe, Nga Tokimatawhaorua, in the canoe house, Waitangi, and the interior of the meeting house on the grounds of the Treaty House at Waitangi.

17

Auckland is not known as the City of Sails for nothing. Marinas dot the bays, none larger than Westhaven, situated within sight of the city centre.

Sightseers head towards Auckland city on one of the many ferries that ply the harbour, while on busy Queen Street a pavement artist attracts a crowd to admire his work.

The city is connected to the North Shore suburbs by the Harbour Bridge, built in 1959, with extra lanes added by Japanese engineers (and wittily referred to as 'the Nippon clip-on').

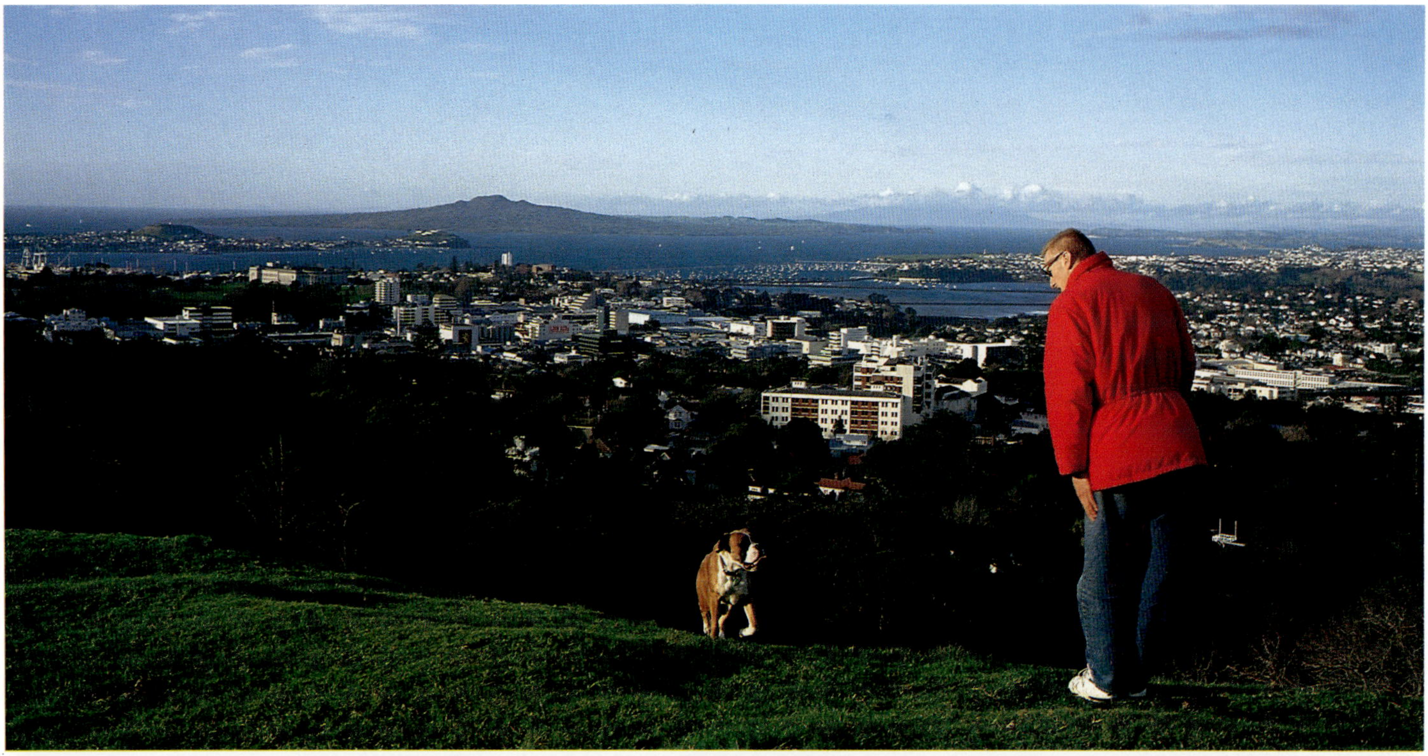

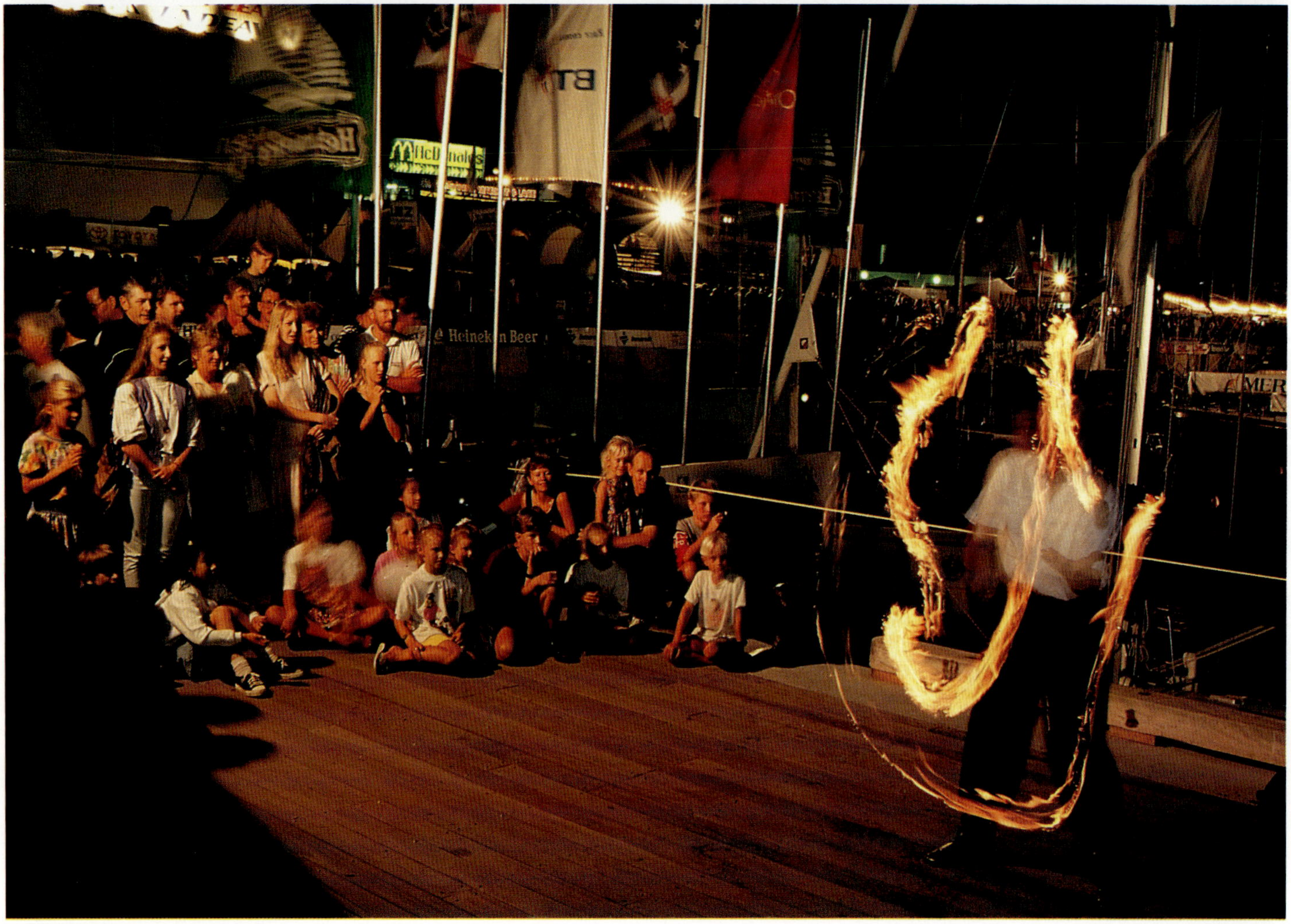
BT
Heineken Beer

From the volcanic cone of Mt Eden the island of Rangitoto provides a sculpted backdrop to the city below. On the waterfront, open air performers delight visitors at any hour of the day or night, while at Kelly Tarlton's Underwater World spectators travel through transparent tunnels within a giant aquarium.

The life of the city. Chic Parnell owes its charm and character to Les Harvey, known to all as Mr Parnell. The Topp Twins are another Auckland institution; a singing duo, they really are twins. Just off Queen Street, Vulcan Lane provides an opportunity to rest one's legs, and perhaps enjoy a fragrant espresso or cappuccino in one of the area's fashionable coffee shops. In the Domain, the Wintergarden provides relaxation of a different kind.

100 PIPERS
RETAIL SPACE
FOR LEASE
PHONE
262-2310
OR
YOUR LOCAL
REAL ESTATE
AGENT
STAMPS
SMIRNOFF
BEELINE LEATHER
ember

The spectacular Marokopa Falls, near Te Anga, in the Waikato.

Waikato to the Volcanic Plateau

During the Land Wars of the 1860s the Maori King Tawhiao threw his hat on a map of New Zealand and said, 'Where the hat lands I will protect all those who have given offence to the Queen of England.' The hat landed on the King Country, an area of limestone, which accounts for its often amazing topography of crags, ravines, canyons and caves. One such formation has become one of the great subterranean wonders of the world — the Waitomo Caves. The spectacular Glow-Worm Grotto shimmers with a million tiny lights like a miniature heaven.

The stronghold of the Maori Kings is in the Waikato on the Turangawaewae marae at Ngaruawahia. Not far away is Taupiri Mountain, where the Maori Kings are buried. Through this landscape winds the mighty Waikato River. Each year in March war canoes sail on the river as part of an annual celebration of Kingitanga, the heritage of the Maori King movement.

Right at the heart of the North Island is the Volcanic Plateau. The volcanic area actually runs from White Island on the east coast diagonally through Rotorua down to Taupo and the mountains of Tongariro National Park.

At Whakarewarewa Village, in Rotorua, Maori culture forms part of a theatrical backdrop of mudpools, hot springs, drifting steam and spouting geysers. If you want to be reminded of a more ferocious aspect of the area visit Waiotapu or the Waimangu Valley. In this region, in 1886, Mount Tarawera erupted, destroying the fabulous Pink and White Terraces. Drive on to Taupo, and when you swim in the lake, go yachting or fish for trout, just remember that once upon a time this was a volcano that blew its top.

A Maori sentinel stands to welcome visitors to the Ohaki Maori village on the approach to the Waitomo Caves.

At Waitomo, in the King Country, sightseers come from all over the world to visit the magnificent Waitomo Caves, one of the world's natural wonders. The traditional boat journey will take you through the caves, or you can join a blackwater rafting tour to explore this underground world in more adventurous fashion.

The city of Rotorua, with its ever-present smell of hydrogen sulphide, is at the heart of a region known for its spectacular volcanic beauty. Among its many attractions is the historic bathhouse in the Government Gardens, home of the Rotorua Art and History Museum. Also of interest is the Agrodome, which regularly features demonstrations of sheep shearing and

dog working. But Rotorua is not only a mecca for tourists; its setting enables locals to enjoy lakeside living beside one of the many lakes in the area.

Rotorua's Whakarewarewa Reserve is a major centre of Maori culture and has become an important school of learning for Maori craftsmen and women. At its entrance visitors practise the hongi, the traditional Maori greeting. The carvings on the meeting house have a special significance for the local people.

The Te Arawa people are well known for their spectacular singing and dancing. Women practise the art of poi dancing and men perform the haka. Traditional stories are told in the movements and actions that accompany the songs.

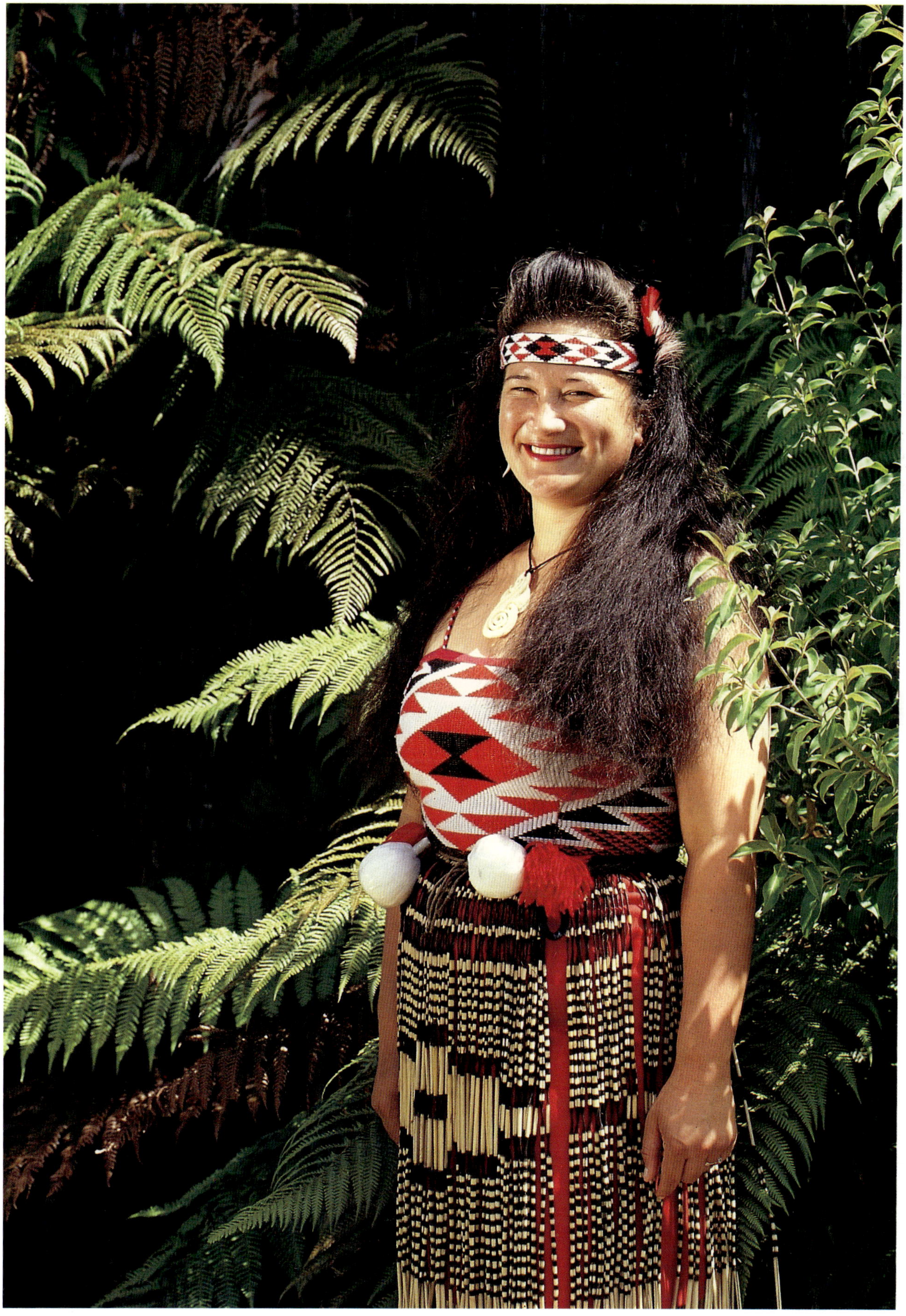

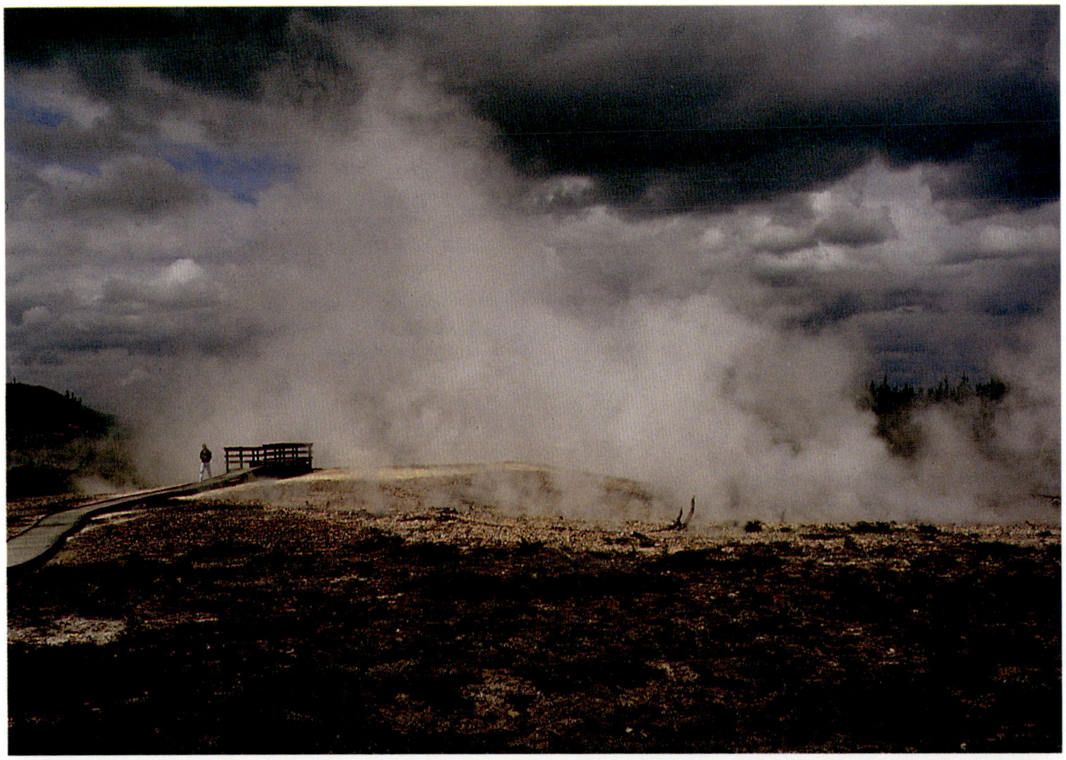

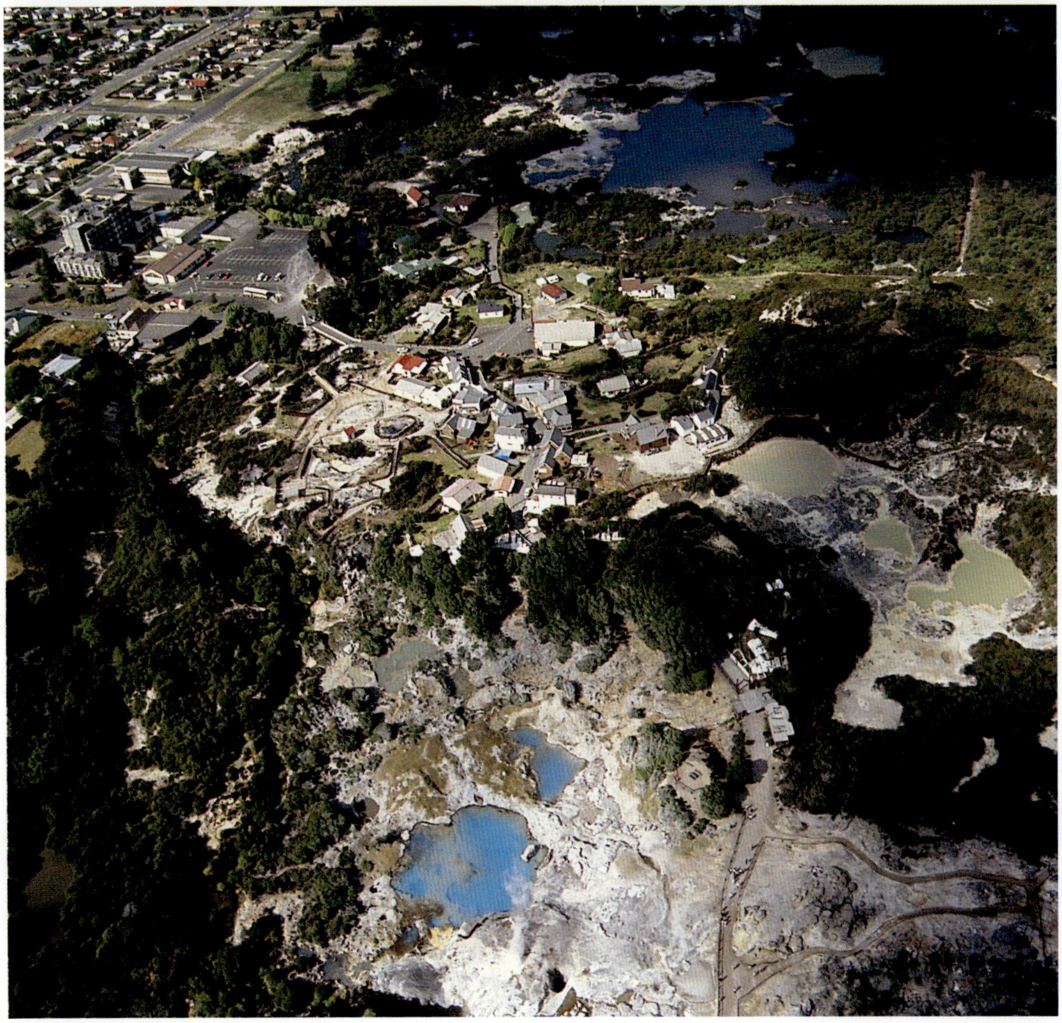

The area around Rotorua boasts an amazing variety of thermal activity. While the geysers and mudpools at Whakarewarewa (opposite, bottom) are well known, a visit to the Wairakei Thermal Valley (opposite, top) just 10 km north of Taupo can provide an equally dramatic experience of steam and bubbling mud. Halfway between Rotorua and Taupo the colourful Champagne Pool (above) is one of the attractions of Waiotapu Scenic Reserve.

Across Lake Tarawera can be seen the famous Mt Tarawera, which on 10 June 1886 exploded, destroying the fabulous Pink and White Terraces.

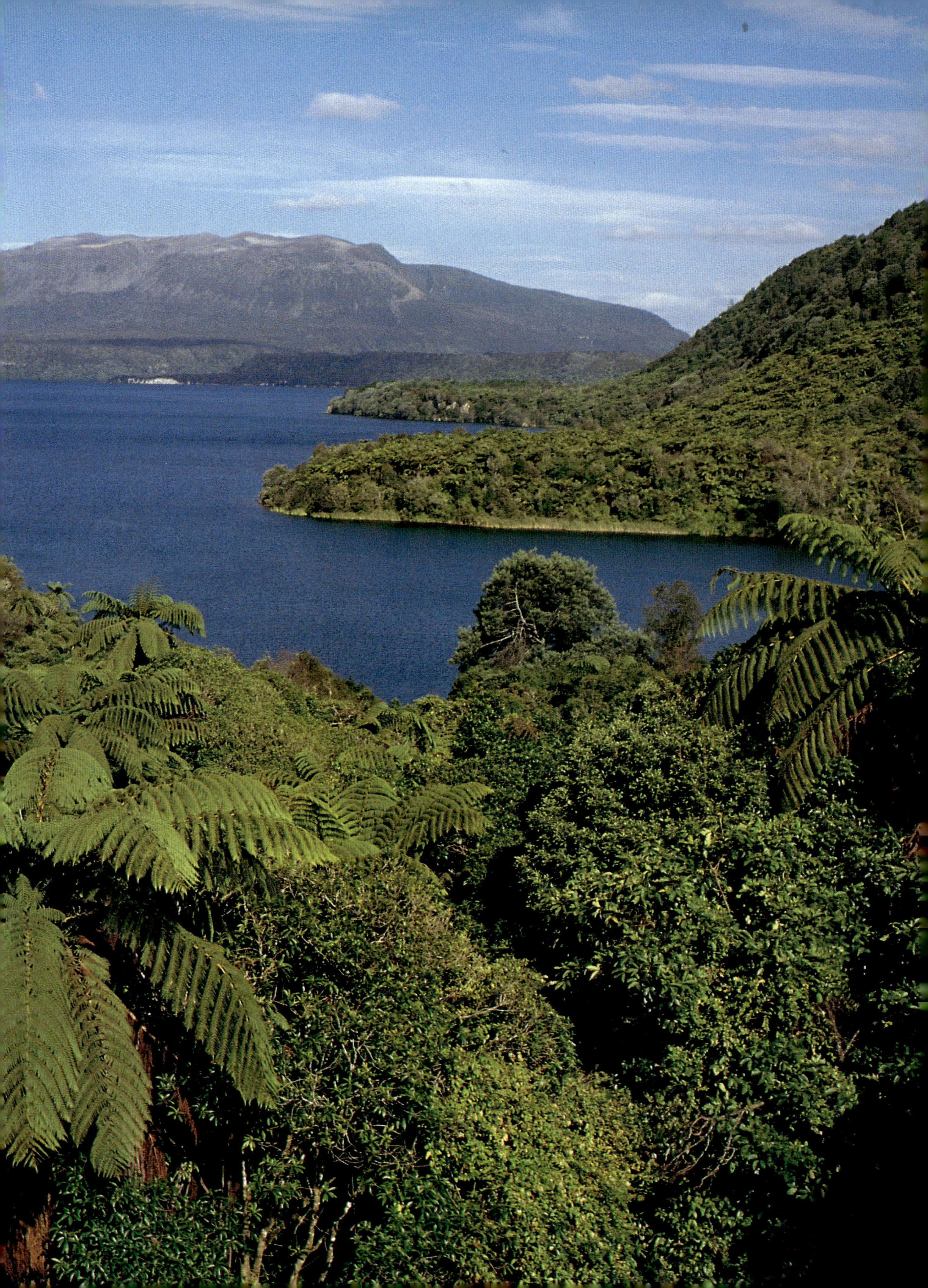

Steam rises from the Wairakei geothermal power station, the second largest in the world. The awesome power of the earth's natural resources can also be seen at the mighty Huka Falls, on the Waikato River, a little nearer Taupo.

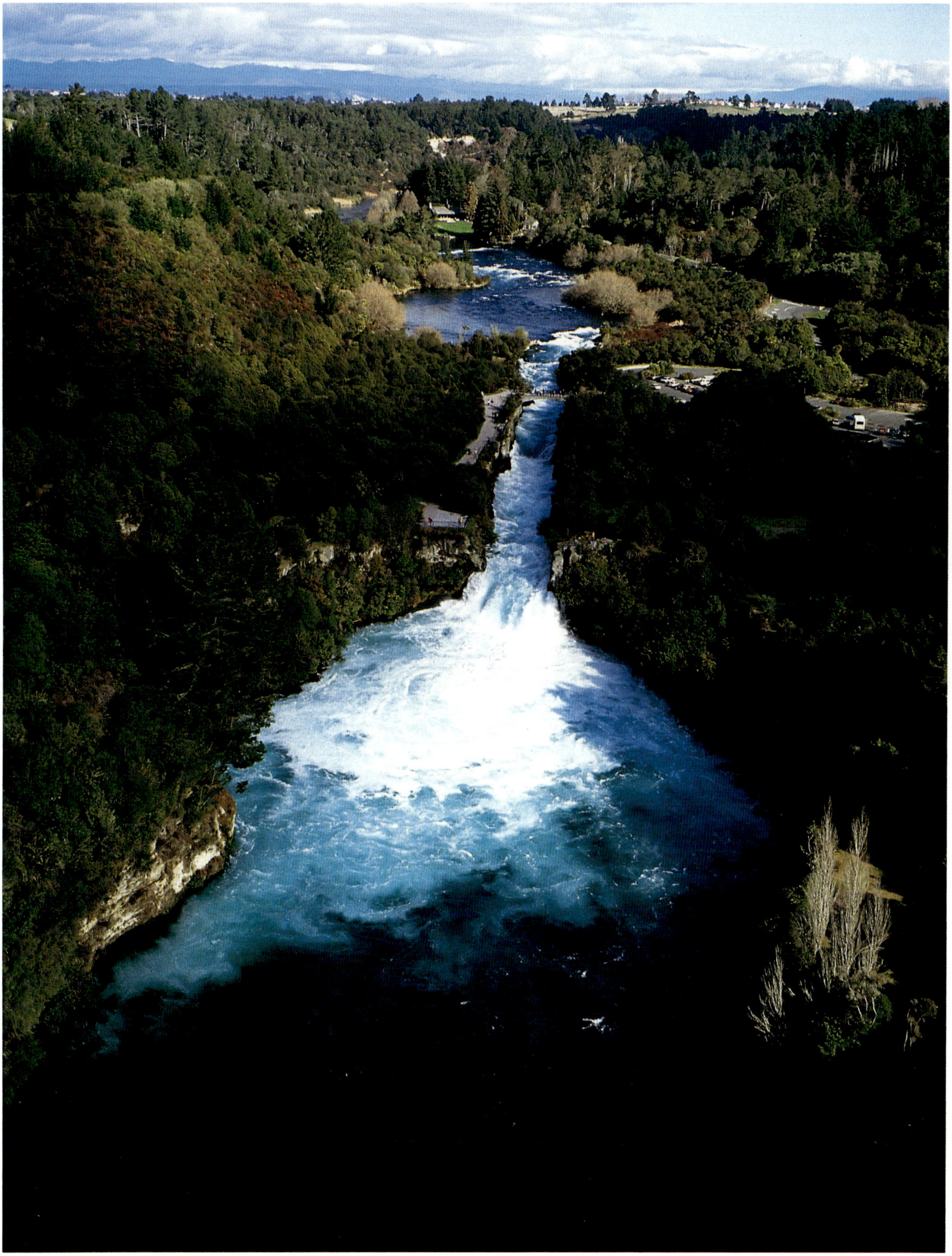

New Zealanders and visitors from all over the world come to fish the waters of Lake Taupo and ski the slopes of Mt Ruapehu, whose warm crater lake looks deceptively quiet in the afternoon sun. Although the mountain has not erupted in recent times, it is still an active volcano. At the foot of the mountain stands The Grand Chateau, with Mt Ngauruhoe beyond.

43

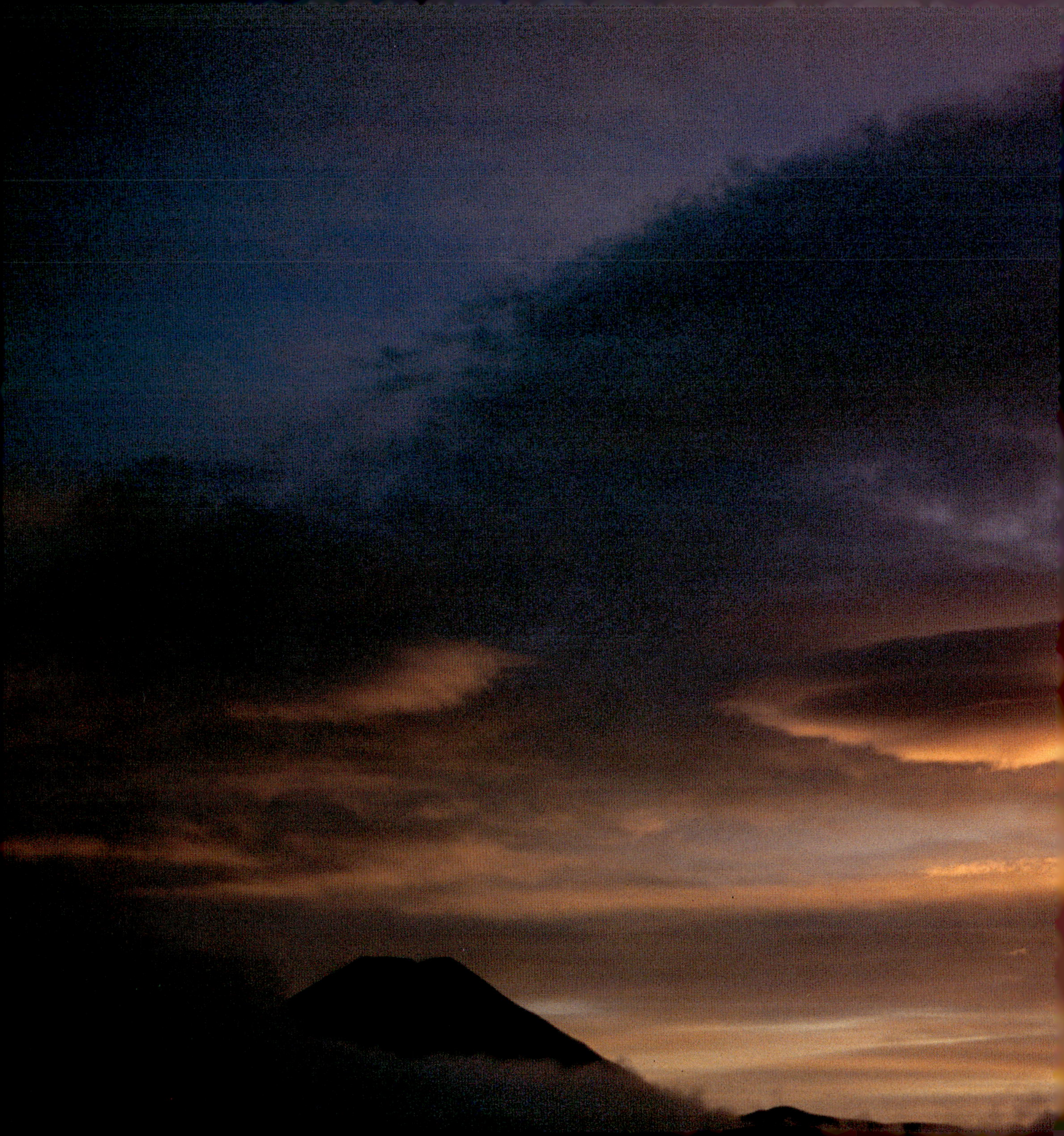

Mt Ngauruhoe at sunrise, obscured by the swirling clouds.

Late afternoon near Port Jackson,
Coromandel Peninsula.

Coromandel to the Wairarapa

Before the coming of the Pakeha, Coromandel provided an impenetrable screen of lush fern and kauri forest. Like the Northland forests, however, the kauri of Coromandel were soon felled for the ship-building industry. Gold was discovered at Thames and Waihi in 1867, and the gold industry flourished until early this century. Today gold is once again being mined at Waihi, but Coromandel is better known for the golden sand of its beaches and the wild beauty of its peninsula.

The shoreline of the Bay of Plenty can take your breath away, especially when pohutukawa blossoms in the summer. When Europeans settled the area it was developed into sheep and cattle country, but today oranges, kiwifruit and grapes have taken over. The harvest is shipped to markets around the world.

South of the Bay of Plenty is East Cape. For a time whaling flourished along the coast, but today's pursuits are primarily fishing, sheep and cattle grazing, and forestry. The settlements haven't changed much since the old days, resembling frontier towns out of a Western movie.

The beaches around the Cape, Poverty Bay and down through Hawke's Bay are among the most magnificent in New Zealand, and the whole coast resonates with history, both Maori and Pakeha. Some of the biggest Maori meeting houses are found here, and some of the North Island's most graceful colonial houses.

Inland from the Cape are the mysterious Ureweras, home of the Tuhoe people, the Children of the Mist. Their kingdom is a mountain fortress guarded by rocky terrain, silver waterfalls and lakes.

Hawke's Bay is the home of some of New Zealand's great sheep stations. More recently its climate has encouraged diversification into horticulture, market gardening and orcharding. Half of New Zealand's wine is made in Hawke's Bay. The twin cities of the area, Napier and Hastings, were severely damaged in an earthquake in 1931. Napier was reconstructed in the angular, jazzy, Art Deco style and today is known as the Art Deco Capital of the World.

Then there's the Wairarapa, the centre of New Zealand's Scandinavian community, and a strong agricultural region. The main city of the Wairarapa is Masterton, while nearby Martinborough is the centre of a growing wine industry.

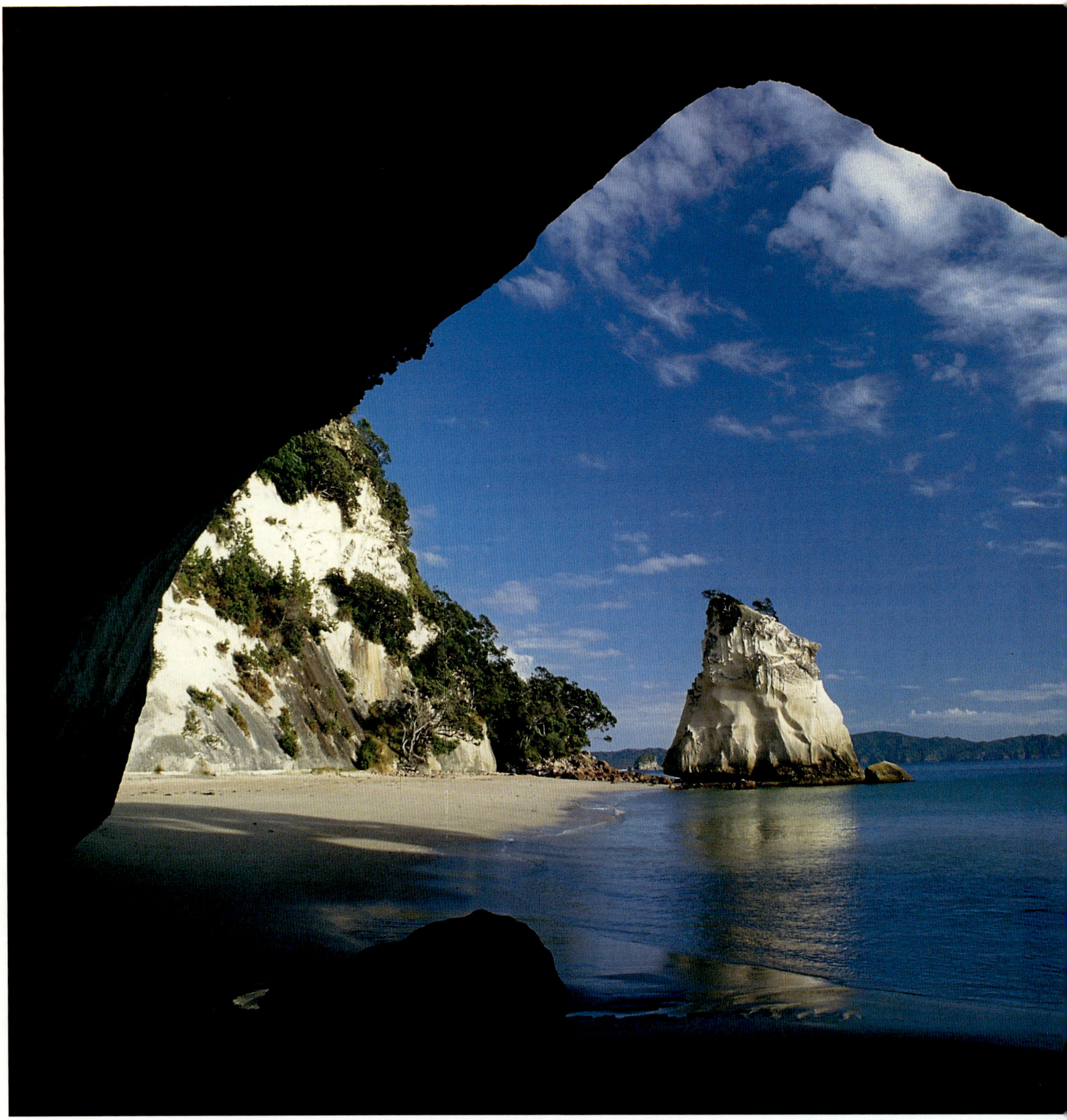

The deserted peace of Cathedral Cove, near Hahei, on the Coromandel Peninsula, contrasts with the gentle clamour of a livestock auction at nearby Coroglen.

Driving Creek railway, the creation of potter Barry Brickell, winds up through the brilliant green of the bush to a view across the Coromandel valley.

The east coast of the Coromandel Peninsula looks straight across the ocean to the place where the sun rises. Here at Opoutere the sunrises are dramatic, with colours ranging from delicate ochres and pinks to cerise, violet and vermillion.

51

The fishing boat *Gay Dolphin* tosses in Coromandel Harbour in a sea quickening with the tide. At Thames memories abound of the gold rushes of the 1860s and '70s, when the town's population reached 20,000, almost twice that of Auckland. The Brian Boru Hotel, one of the few remaining accommodation houses, is best known today for its Murder Mystery weekends.

53

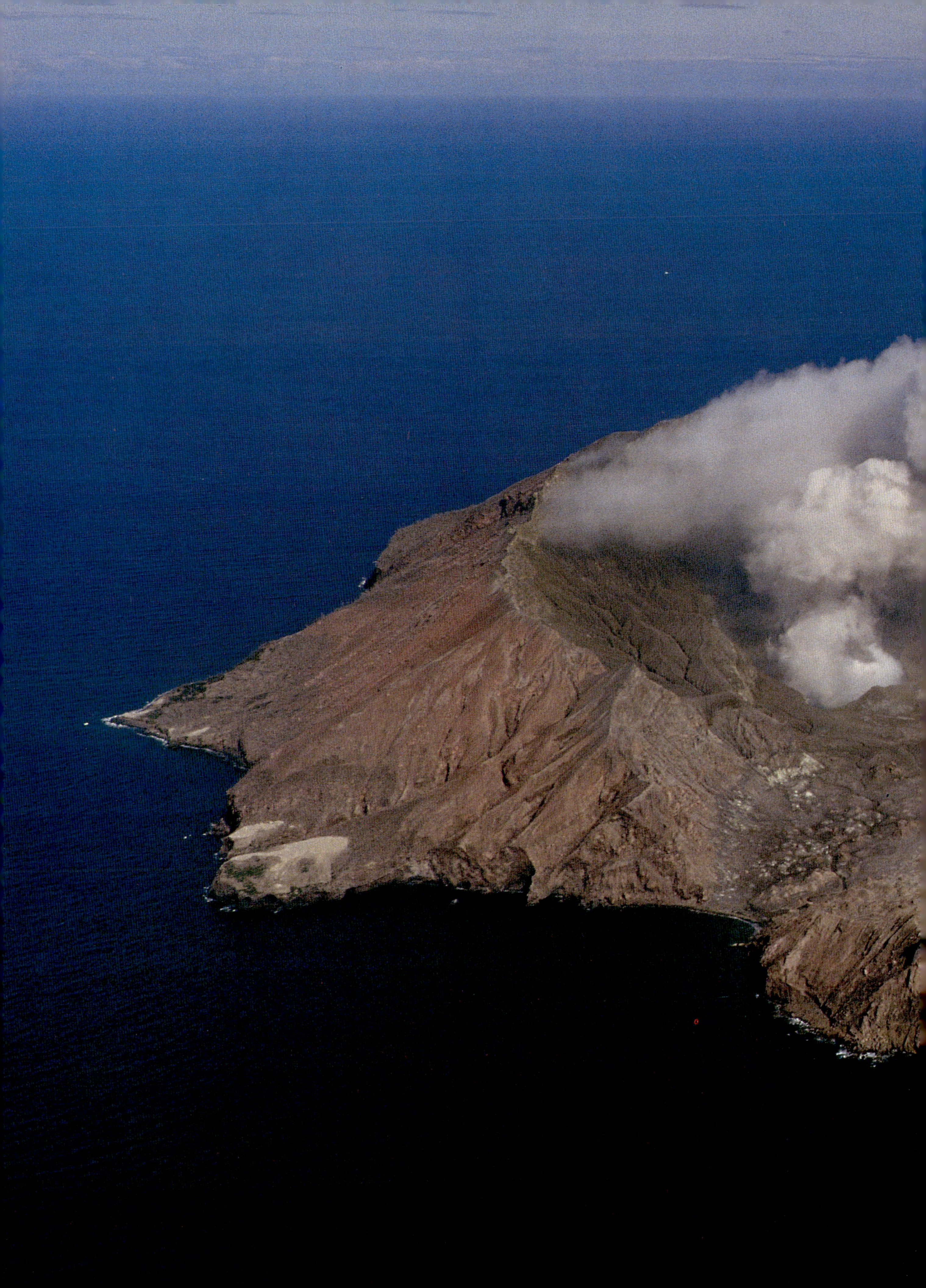

White Island, in the Bay of Plenty, occasionally sends up steam and lava just to remind us that it is still an active volcano.

Mt Maunganui, famous for its surf, is a favourite summer holiday spot in the sunny Bay of Plenty.

On the wall of a fish and chip shop at Katikati, a family poses outside a typical Bay of Plenty church, as if waiting for a photograph to be taken. On the beach near Opotiki, two Maori seek the succulent pipi, a shellfish regarded as a delicacy.

57

The East Coast has a relaxed lifestyle, and the drive around the coast is for those with plenty of time, who are happy to leave themselves open to whatever happens next. The locals usually have time for a friendly chat. During cultural practice at Apanui School, Te Kaha, a young girl grins with enjoyment and fun, and boys try to come to grips with the finer points of the haka.

59

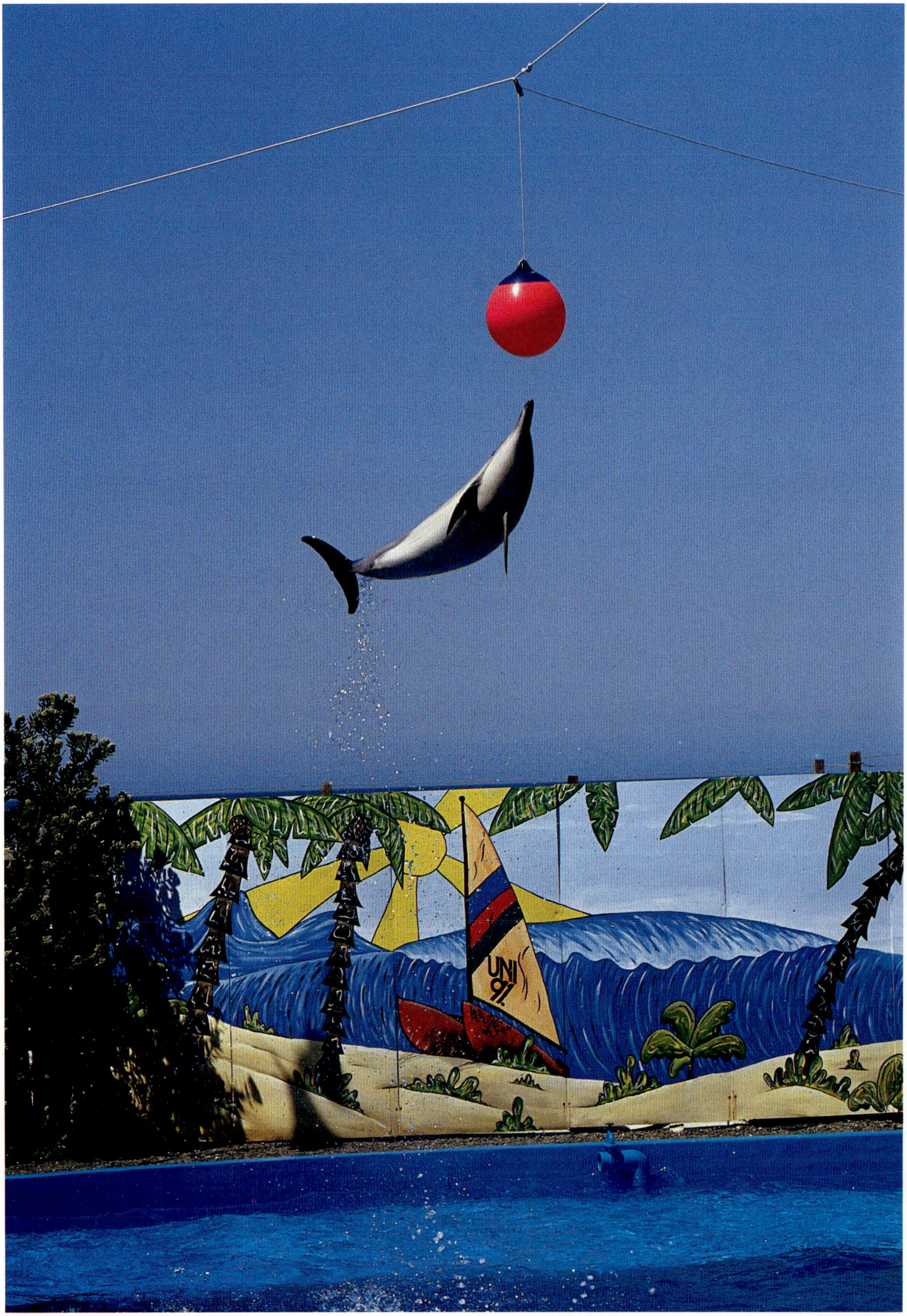
UNI
91.

A dolphin leaps during a sea world display at Marineland, Napier, one of several attractions on the city's waterfront. Cape Kidnappers, a short drive from Napier, is home to a colony of about 5,000 gannets. Some people walk around the coast to the colony; others prefer to be driven all the way.

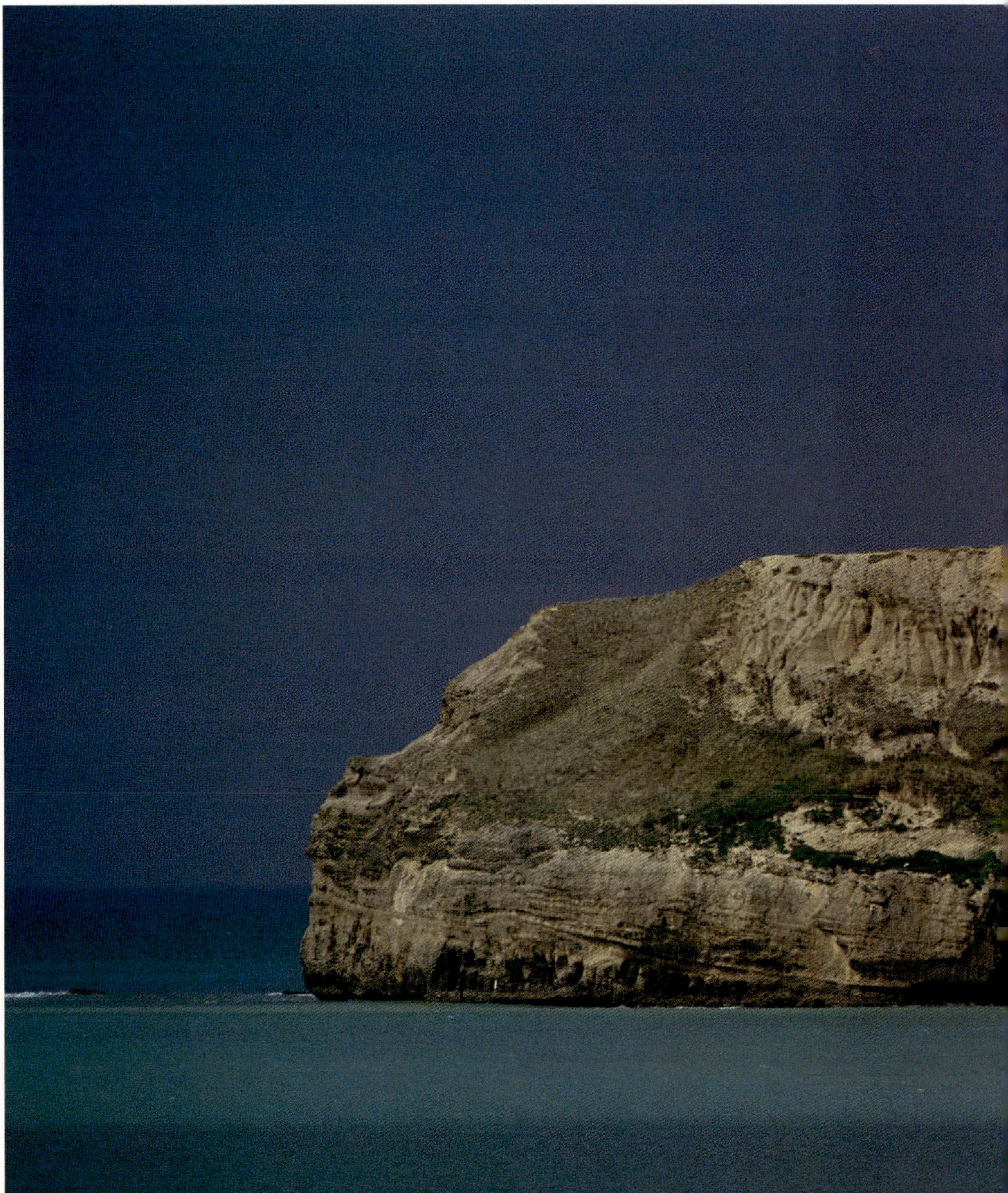

Castlepoint Lighthouse, east of Masterton, signals a warning to ships off the wild Wairarapa coast. A fishing boat shelters in the lee of the headland.

Two trampers in Whanganui National Park, near the Bridge to Nowhere.

Taranaki to Wellington

On a clear day, Taranaki (also known as Mt Egmont) can be seen from the South Island. It made itself known to the earliest Maori canoe voyagers but when Abel Tasman sailed past in 1642 it hid itself from him. However, for James Cook in 1770 Taranaki was kinder. He saw it through cloud and rain, with lightning dancing around its crown. In 1841 ships of the New Zealand Company arrived from England's Plymouth and, within the gaze of Taranaki, established the settlement of New Plymouth.

From the summit of Taranaki you feel as if you can see the world. Ruapehu, Taranaki's brother mountain, is eastward. Seaward is a curve of black sand, like a fin flicking at the deep blue of the Tasman Sea. Below, the rainforest carpets the flanks of the mountain, and beyond the plains roll towards New Plymouth and Hawera to the south. Offshore, oil rigs dot the Taranaki Bight.

To the south, the deep gorges, waterfalls and wilderness of the Whanganui River have a special attraction for those who would explore it by canoe, white-river raft or jetboat. The Rangitikei and Manawatu rivers, further inland, are just as stunning. At the seaward end of the Manawatu gorge is the largest city of the plains, Palmerston North. For many years a university town, today Palmerston North is also a centre for agricultural and horticultural research, and for wider education.

Wellington, the capital, is one of New Zealand's most cultured and vibrant cities. The suburbs of Wellington all retain their own special character. Newtown, for example, is a mix of Maori, Pacific Island, Greek and new immigrant families, creating a joyful blend of fun and excitement. In recent years the waterfront and inner city have been transformed into a showcase of art, music, theatre and culture. Innovative architecture has added a new and exciting look to the city, contrasting with the older, gentler areas of Mount Victoria and Tinakori Road.

Mt Taranaki, also known as Mt Egmont, is New Zealand's most climbed mountain and the centrepiece of Egmont National Park. The mountain is a volcanic cone, sculpted into its present shape by past eruptions. Below the steep upper slopes dark forest takes over, in turn giving way to the softer colours of the Taranaki farmland.

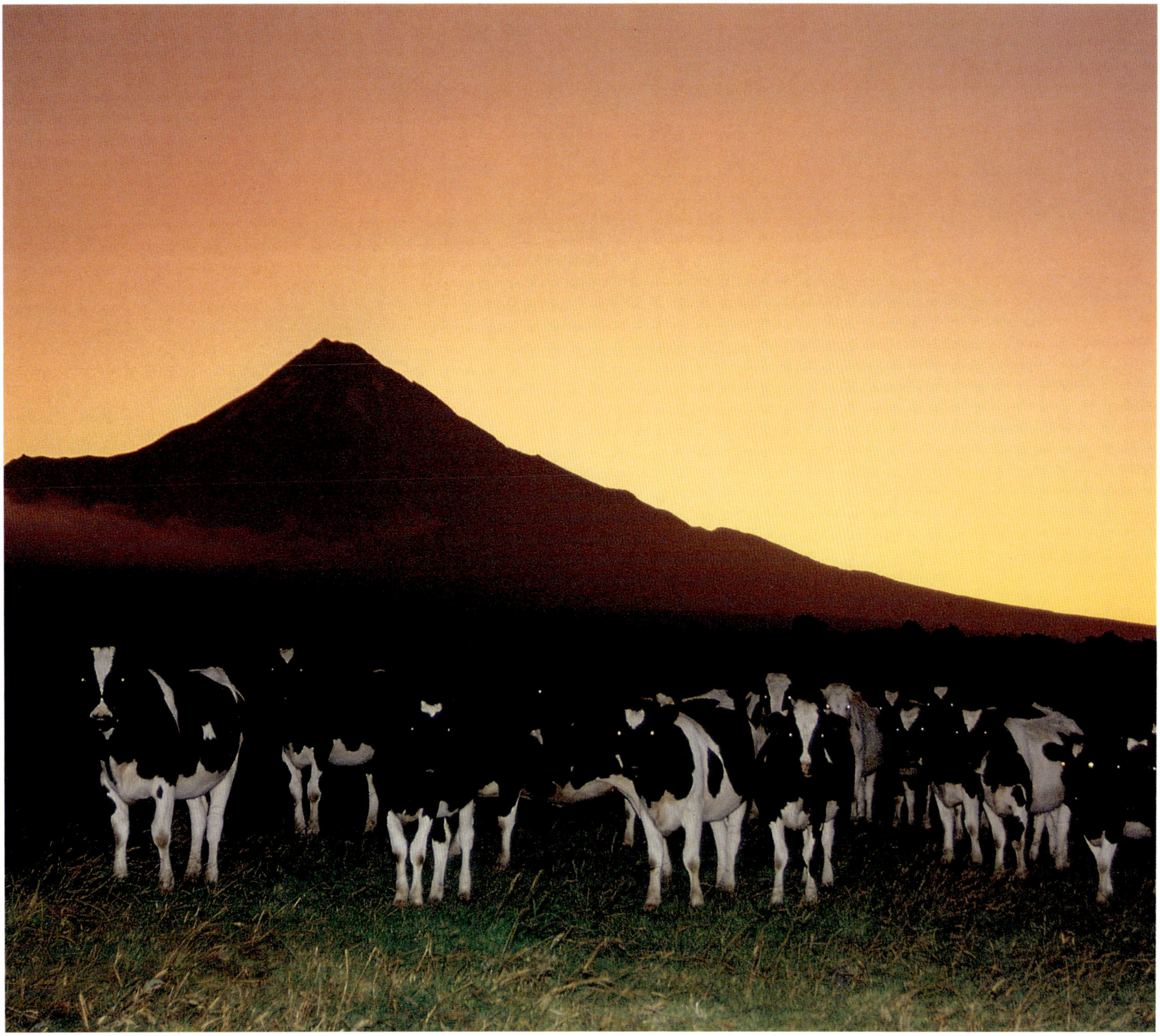

Whanganui National Park, which opened in 1987, encompasses 79,000 hectares of lowland forest on both sides of the Whanganui River. The Park is popular with trampers, many of whom head for the Bridge to Nowhere. Built in 1936, the bridge was never fully utilised as many settlers were abandoning the area by the time of its completion. Today the area's main industry is tourism, and the river provides exciting jet-boating and canoeing adventures.

69

Low sun illuminates Oriental Bay, one of Wellington's most attractive suburbs.

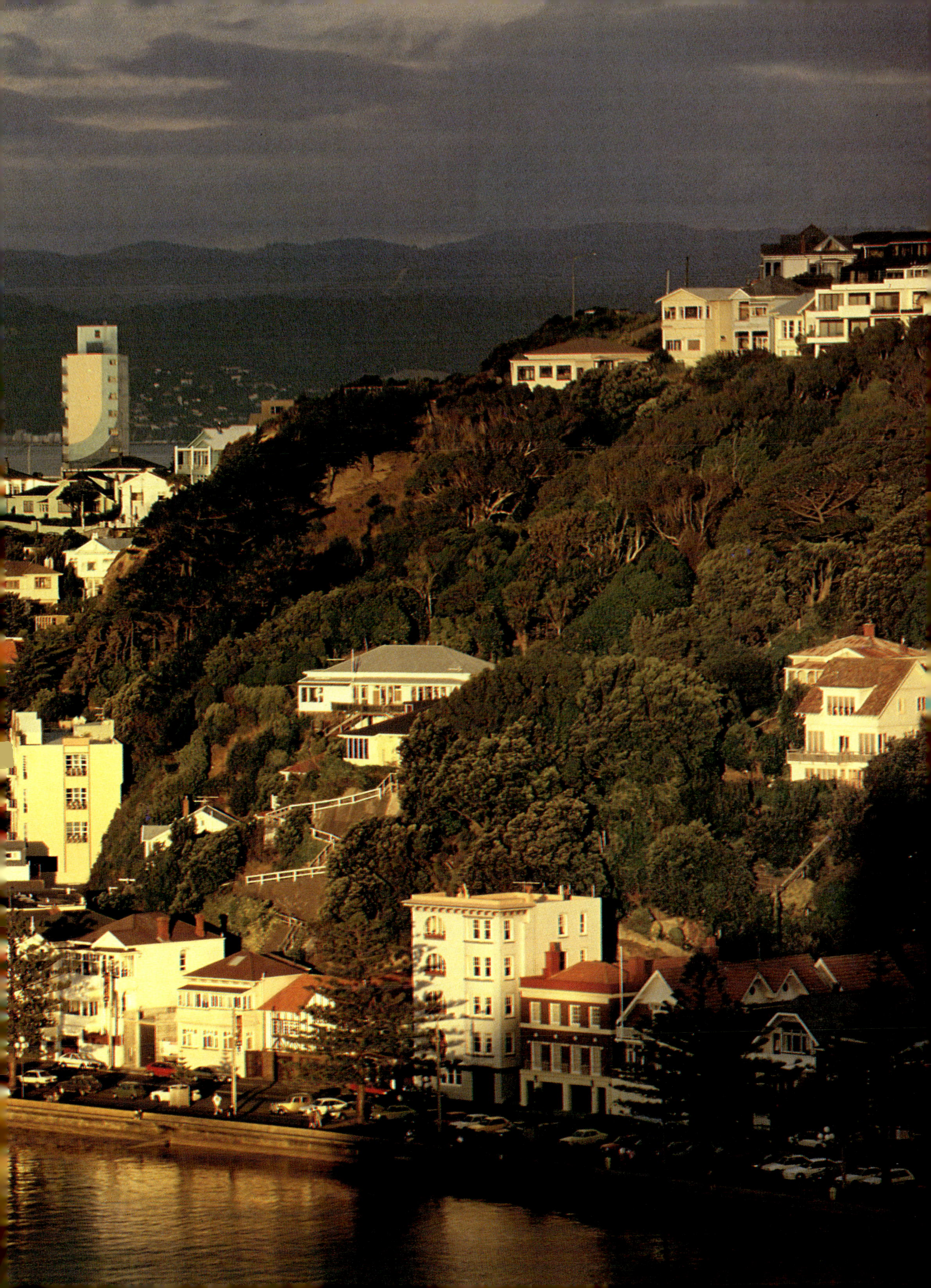

Wellington's Beehive is an addition to the old Parliament Buildings. Opened in 1981, it was inspired, so people say, by the logo on a box of matches.

The Cable Car provides a swift, steep ride from the inner city, seen here from Tinakori Hill, to the university suburb of Kelburn.

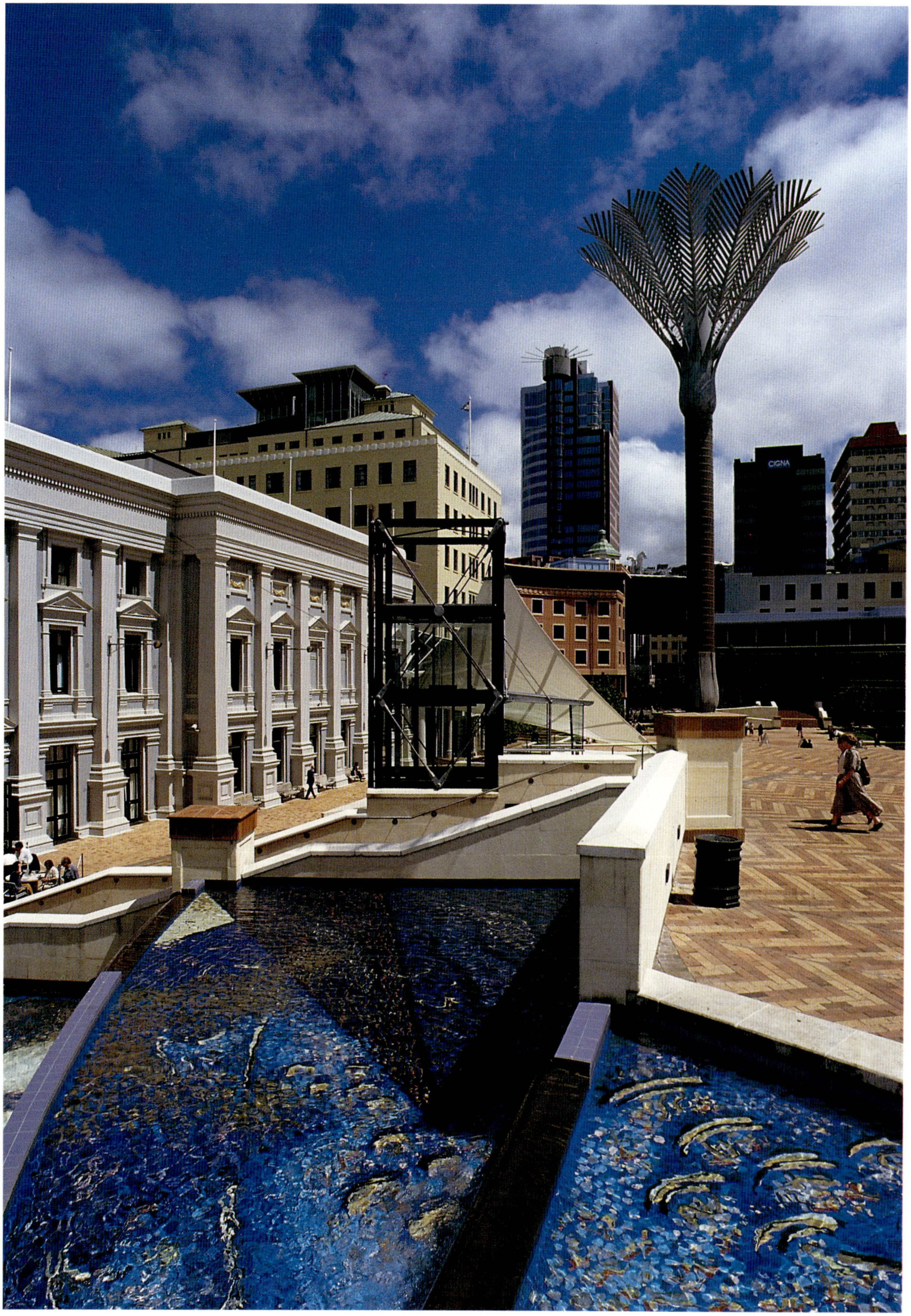
CIGNA

The Wellington skyline has been transformed in recent years, with a number of striking new buildings. Wellingtonians are particularly proud of their Civic Square, with its paved courtyard and tiled fountains. The metallic nikau palm is one of several that surround the Wellington City Library. The library's curvilinear glass walls reflect light from a tiled pool.

The Marlborough Sounds offer glorious isolation, a calm haven in which to escape from the pressures of the world.

Marlborough and Nelson to Kaikoura

The Marlborough Sounds are magical sea-filled valleys which provide spectacular sailing and swimming. Their shores are clothed with unspoilt bush. Some of the islands further out are home to New Zealand's tuatara, a living link back to the dinosaurs of old.

Inland from the Sounds, the perspective changes. High tussock and alpine country overlook gentle river valleys and the sprawling Wairau Plains. Marlborough was once the home of great sheep stations, but today orchards, vineyards and berry fields dominate the landscape. The soil, and the sun, are particularly conducive to fine wine production and as a result Marlborough is home to some of New Zealand's best, and biggest, wineries.

West of Marlborough is Nelson, described by Abel Tasman in 1642 as 'a great land uplifted high'. Nelson shares with Blenheim one of the best climates in the country. Its beaches are golden sand swept by sparkling sea, the townships are colourful and friendly, and fruit trees, vines and berries flourish amid valleys of trees and ferns.

Nelson City, established by the New Zealand Company in 1842, is the centre of the province. Today it is a delightful mix of modernity and old world charm. Although its traditional industry remains horticulture, the area's rich fishing grounds have now turned Nelson into the biggest fishing port in New Zealand. The city is also a magnet for artisans — jewellers, potters, glassworkers and sculptors — who create some of New Zealand's finest craftworks. Close by is Abel Tasman National Park, a wonderful area of golden beaches, steep granite formations, limestone caves and native forest.

The Kaikoura coast follows the Pacific seaboard all the way down to Canterbury. Whaling was once a major industry along the coast. Today, the more gentle art of whalewatching provides an opportunity to witness some of the world's most beautiful creatures.

78

The hills surrounding the Marlborough Sounds are dotted with holiday homes, many of them reached by boat. During the still evenings the area is alive with the sounds of sea and forest. Among the most distinctive songsters of the region is the weka, a small flightless bird about the size of a domestic hen.

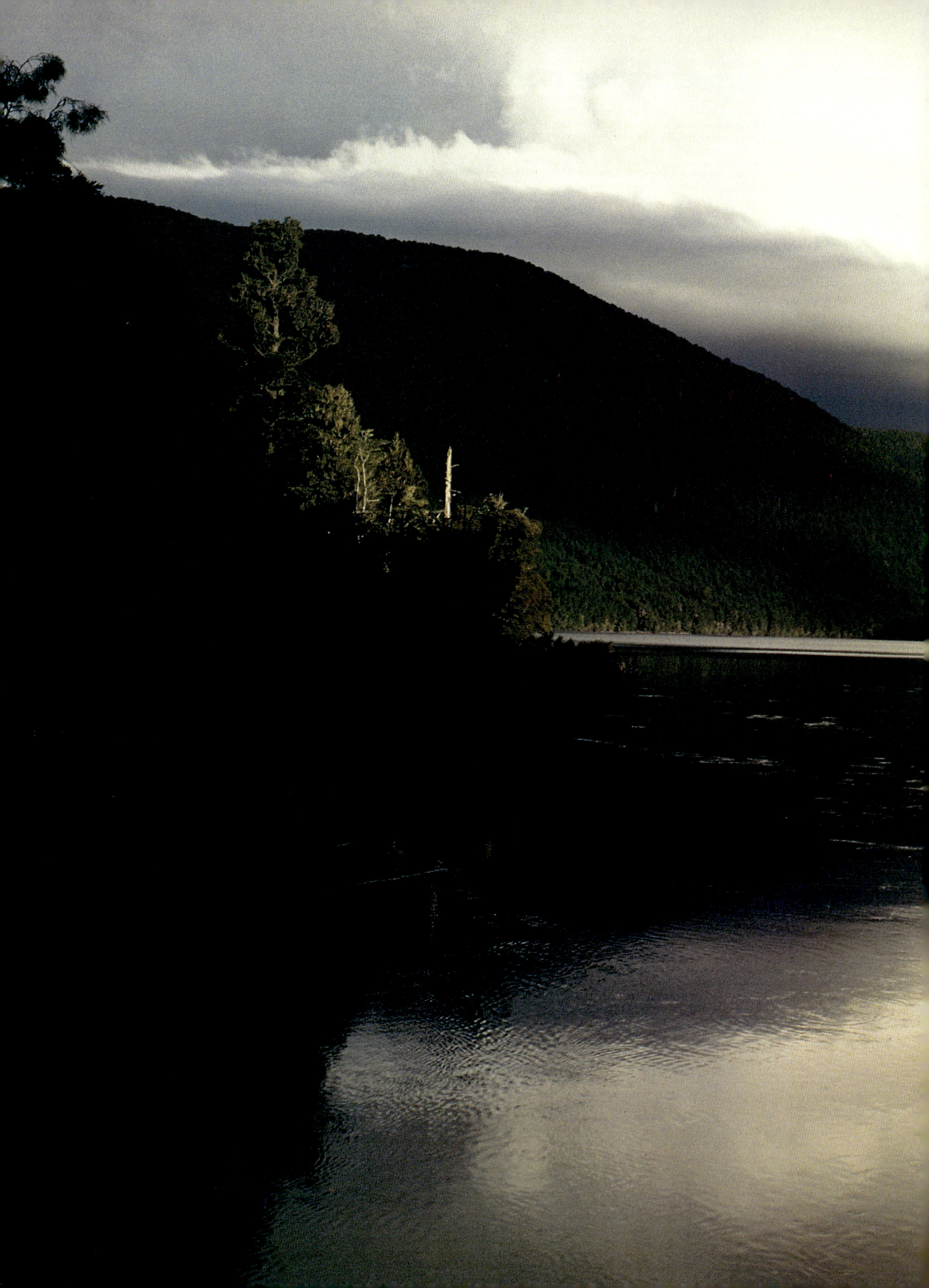

Lake Rotoroa, the larger of the two lakes of Nelson Lakes National Park.

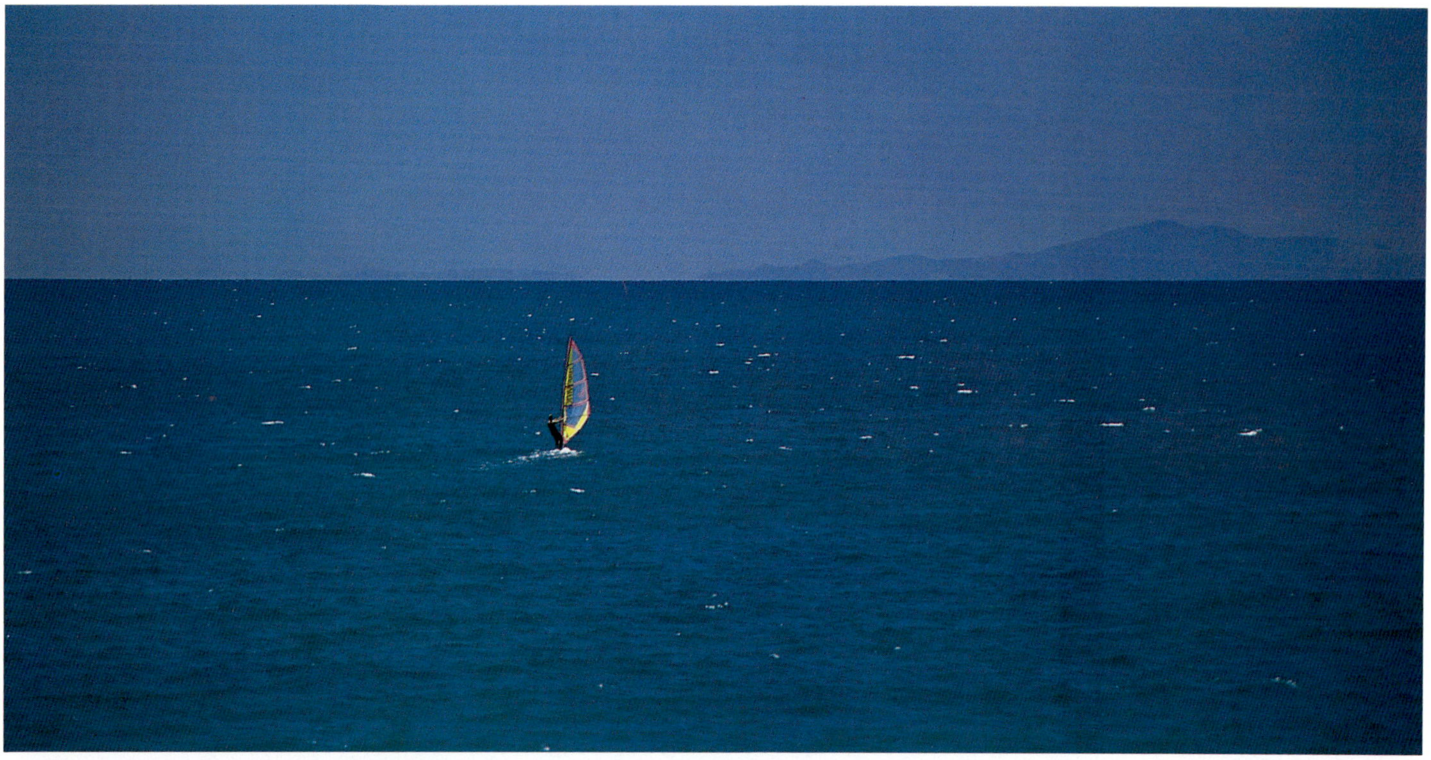

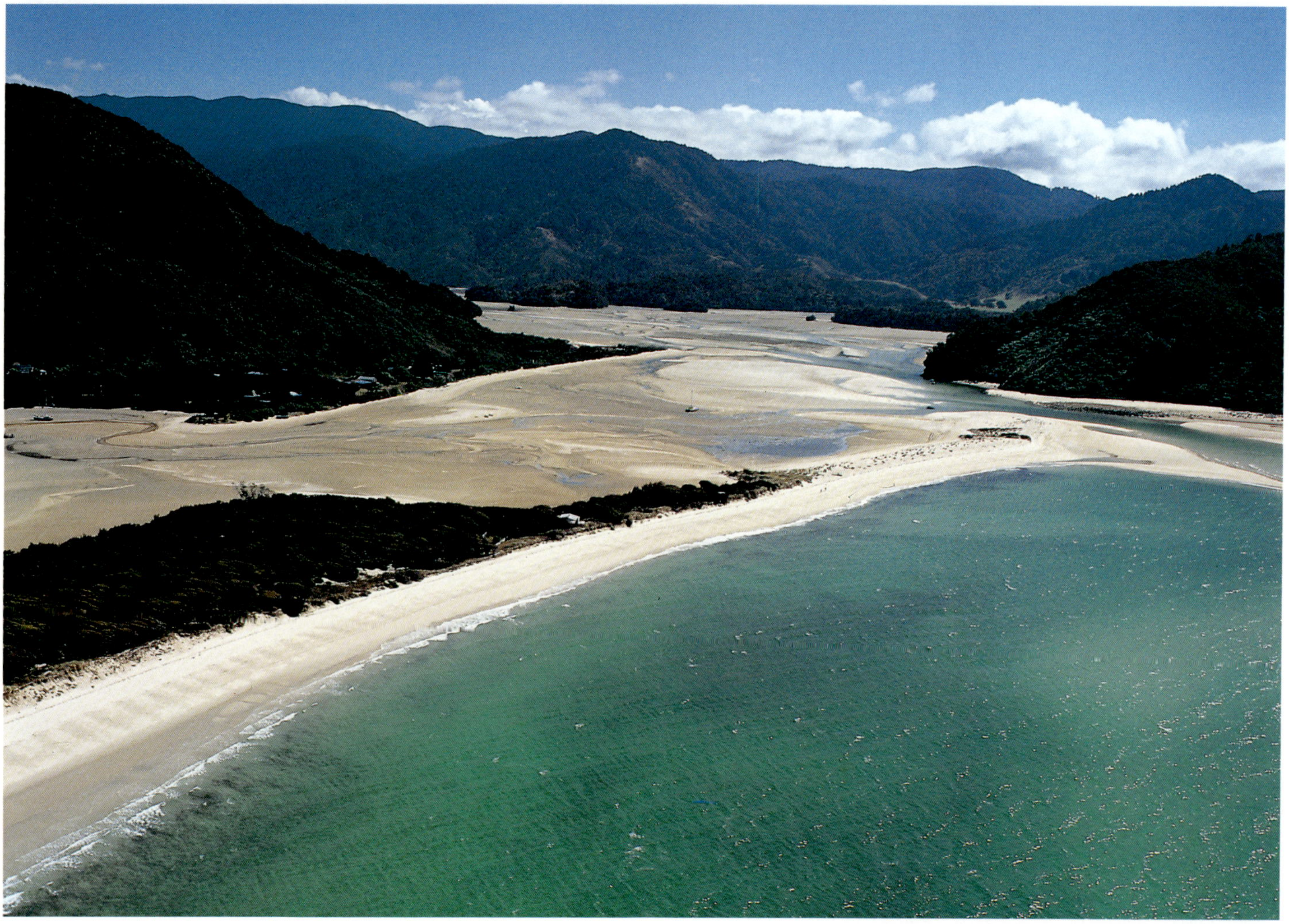

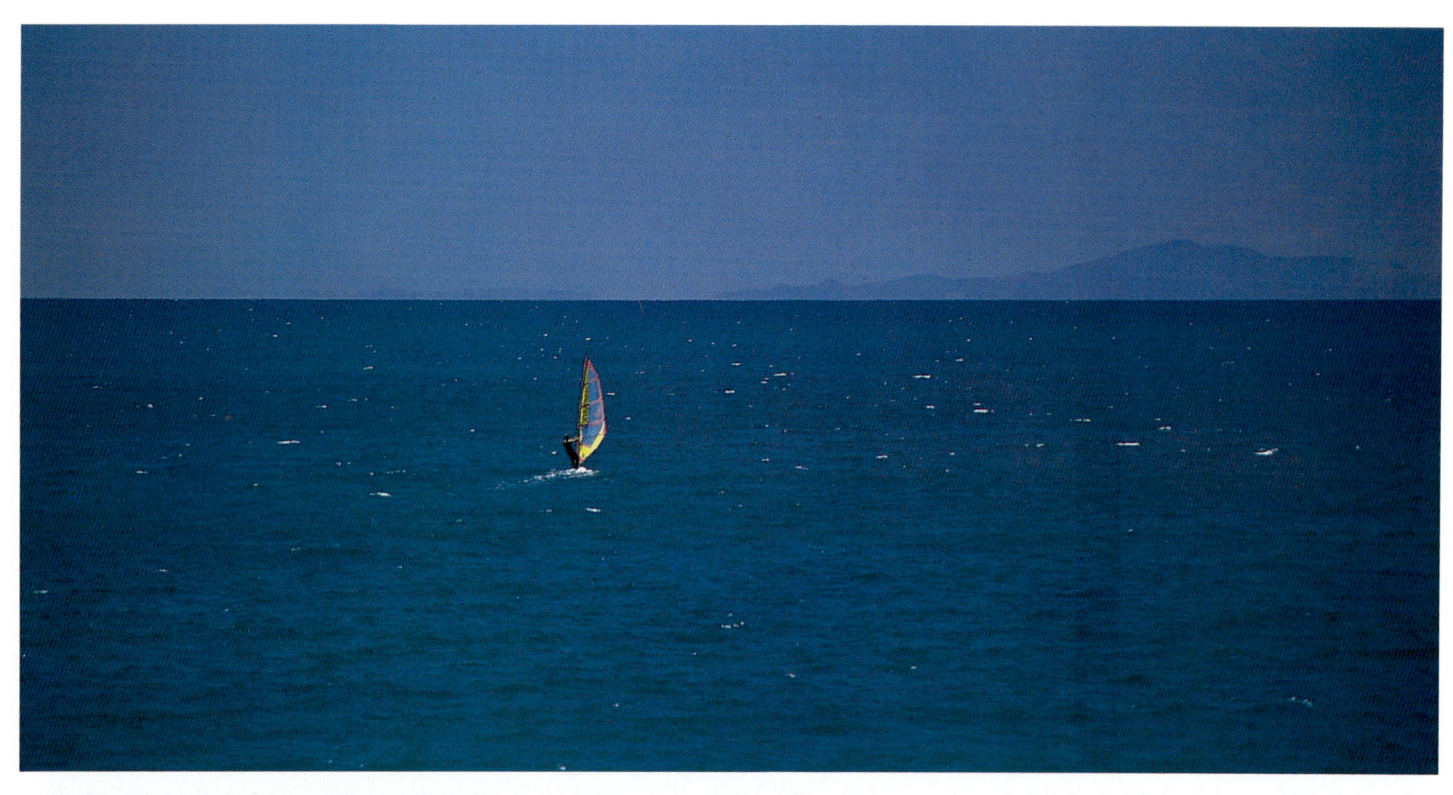

The sun, surf and wind make Abel
Tasman National Park ideal for
yachting, windsurfing and sea kayaking,
or simply lazing on its lovely beaches.

84

Many who visit Kaikoura come by train, enjoying the scenic coastal route. The area is famous for its kai moana, or seafood.

The view from Mount Fyffe, named after a pioneer whaler. Today it is whale watching that draws visitors to Kaikoura, as well as adventure activities such as paragliding.

87

Farmland falls to sea at Akaroa
Harbour, Banks Peninsula.

Christchurch and Canterbury

The landscape of Canterbury is dominated by its mountains. They are sentinels of the southern sky, with passes like narrow gateways through to the West Coast. For the traveller they provide an everchanging vista of immense power and beauty. New Zealand's longest glacier, the Tasman, is located in Mt Cook National Park. Ski-planes regularly set down skiers at the top of the glacier for a fabulous run down a magical river of ice and snow.

The immense Canterbury Plains, once the home of the giant moa, seem to roll on forever. From the air, the plains look like a vast pastoral ocean of patchwork green and gold, interrupted every now and then by the blue-grey of an intricately braided river.

In 1840 the French established a settlement at Akaroa, on Banks Peninsula, a township which today still maintains a piquant Gallic flavour. But it wasn't until 1848 and the establishment of the Canterbury Association in London that the idea of founding an Anglican settlement in New Zealand was formulated. Two years later, in 1850, four ships — the *Randolph, Charlotte Jane, Cressy* and *Sir George Seymour* — landed at Lyttelton. The idea was to transpose a model English society, complete with bishop, gentry, tradespeople and other workers, people known for their respectability and high morals. The result was a South Seas version of Britain that has no parallel in New Zealand.

Nowhere is this more apparent than in Christchurch, the largest city of the South Island. The cathedral triumphs in the centre, and church spires spike the sky. Amid drifting willows the river Avon wends its way through a city of Gothic architecture and ever-changing colours. The green banks and parks blossom with flowers in spring, transforming the city into a colourful garden. Walk around the old university buildings, now transformed into an Arts Centre, or visit some of the city's older schools, splendid amid leafy settings, and you would think you were in an English university town.

There is, of course, also a 'new' Christchurch, vibrant and ambitious, which reminds you quite firmly that the city is looking very much to the future. A busy airport, a growing reputation as an industrial city utilising the best of modern technology, and progressive city planning have made Christchurch one of the most positive of New Zealand's cities.

Cambridge? No, punting on the River Avon, Kiwi-style. The river winds its way through the city of Christchurch, past the modern Town Hall with its ingenious fountain, and the nearby Floral Clock.

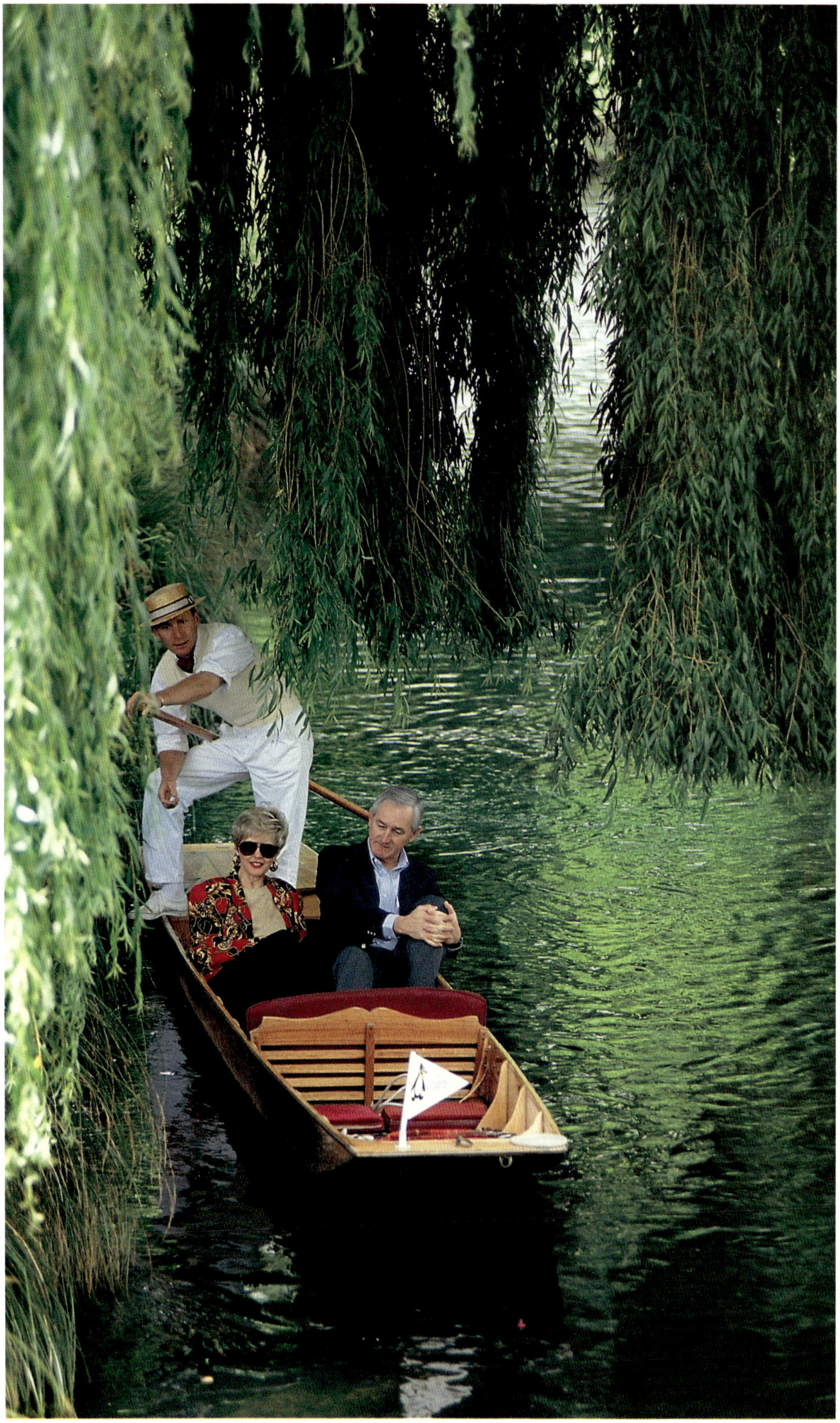

Christchurch's Cathedral Square is always alive with activity. Buskers entertain, people sit and watch the crowds pass by, and the city's Wizard declaims.

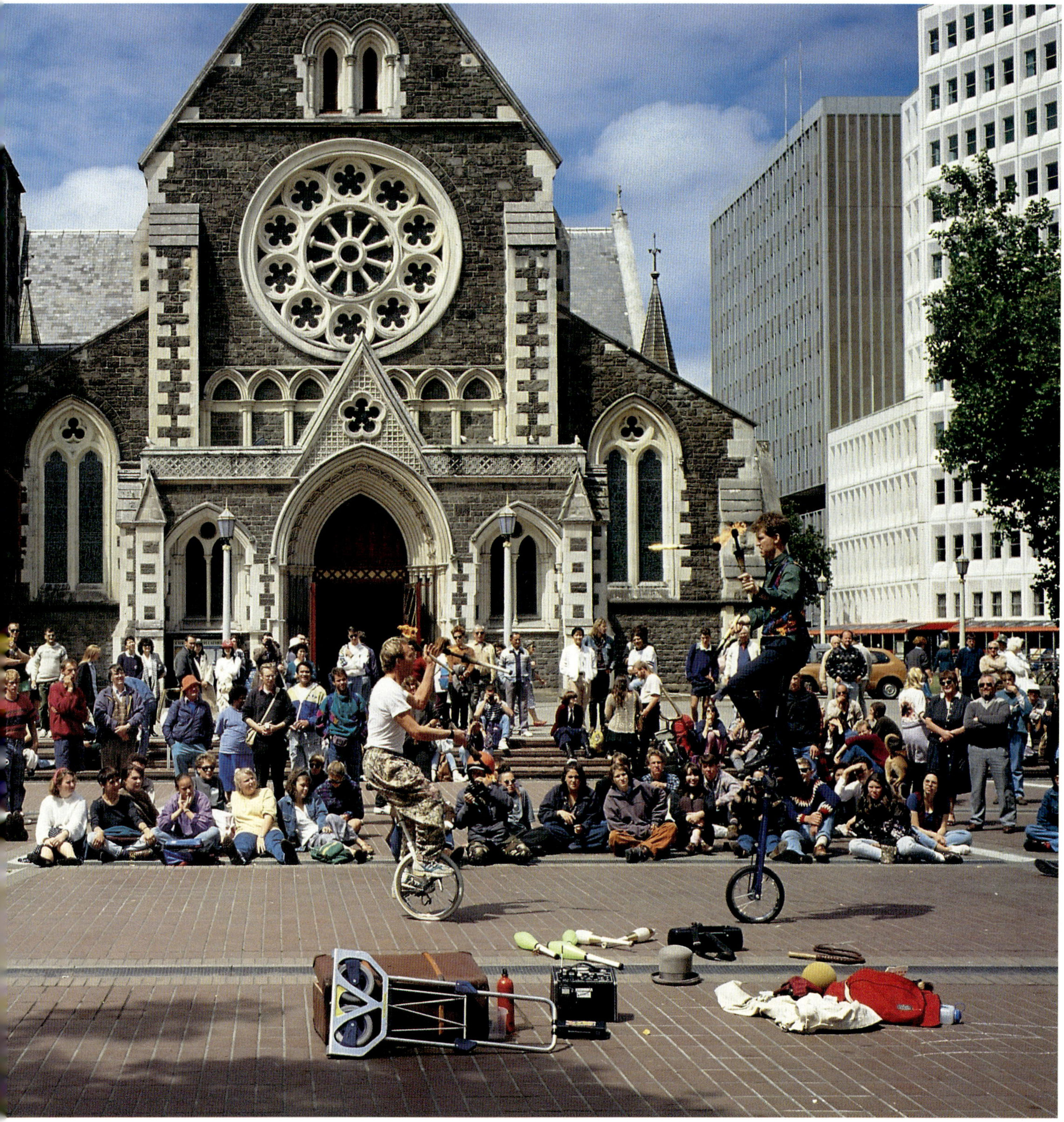

A prominent landmark in Lyttelton is the Timeball Station, its Victorian mechanism signalling the time to ships in the harbour by the dropping of a ball down the mast on the top of the tower.

Christ's College, founded on the principles of an English public school, is one of the country's oldest.

Two cyclists on Summit Road, the rim of the Port Hills, watch the sun set over Christchurch.

95

A large mural, painted on the side of the Fire Station at Lake Tekapo, acknowledges the place of sheep in the colourful history of the Mackenzie country.

The Church of the Good Shepherd, at Lake Tekapo, was built in acknowledgement of the sacrifices of the early runholders of the area. The sheepdogs of the Mackenzie country are also honoured here.

Sheep graze on winter pasture beside Lake Tekapo, South Canterbury.

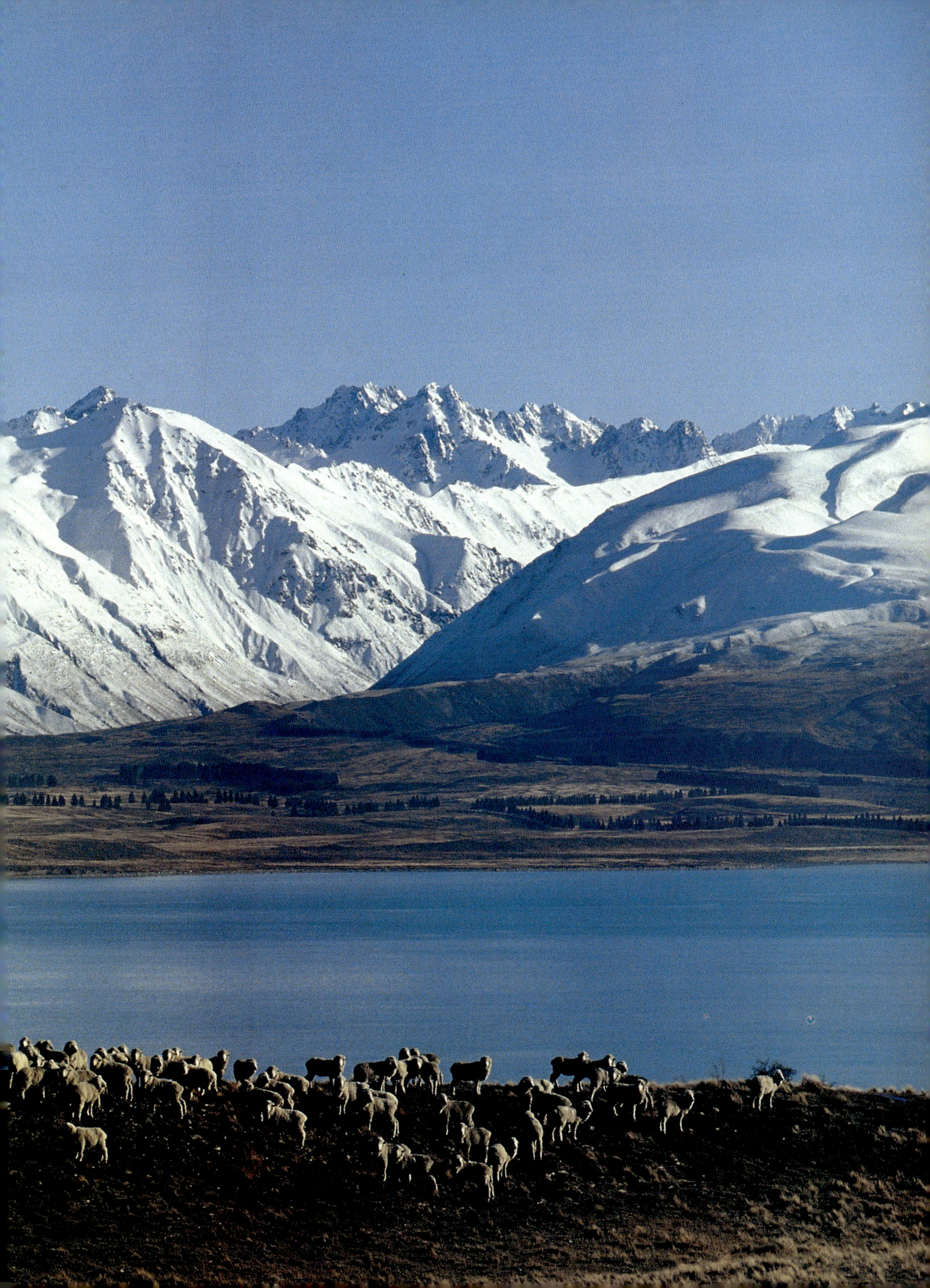

Scenic flights over the Alps are popular. A plane appears as a tiny speck of colour above the vastness of the mighty Tasman Glacier, and a helicopter lands at the head of the glacier.

Mt Cook National Park covers 70,000 hectares of the Southern Alps, and 65 kilometres of mountain chains.

102

From the snow-capped peaks and glaciers, water drains into the braided rivers on both sides of the Main Divide, and forms lakes such as Pukaki, a vital part of the Upper Waitaki Power Development Scheme.

A glimpse of what lies ahead, the coastline of the West Coast.

The West Coast

The West Coast is rather like a forest fortress, its mountain peaks palisades guarding against all-comers. A constant curtain of rain provides an extra layer of protection. Were it not for the fabled greenstone, or pounamu, perhaps the Maori would never have come here, to the great Westland rivers, the Arahura and the Taramakau.

Later, another kind of stone, gold, brought Europeans into the area. Ironically, the gold was found beneath a greenstone boulder by Maori who were more interested in the pounamu. This was in 1864. A year later gold mining began in Hokitika and Reefton. Even later, another mineral, coal, added to the region's prosperity.

The goldmining days brought a sense of the frontier to the West Coast. Perhaps it is because of this that Coasters are considered different from other New Zealanders. Not any better or worse, just a bit different — irreverent, enterprising, sometimes stubborn, but always decent. In many respects they are the archetypal 'good keen men' and independent women of New Zealand's ideal society, having a healthy disrespect for authority and relying more on their own sense of what's right and what isn't.

One of the most dominant features of the West Coast is the opalescent sea, which seems to carry on a constant love affair with the coast. The whole of the West Coast is a place of whispers, of sounds and mysteries, offering moments of sheer beauty as when a white heron feathers the air at its nesting place at Okarito.

It is also a place of immense silence. The beaches are unpopulated and the emerald green forests are isolated. Nowhere is the silence more profound than at the two rivers of ice — the Fox and Franz Josef Glaciers. Sometimes, in the gleaming half-light of day, they defy reality and render the surrounding landscape unreal also.

The astonishing Pancake Rocks, at Punakaiki, lie within one of New Zealand's newest national parks, Paparoa. Nearby the rich red of the pohutukawa flower adds a vivid splash of colour to the bush. A little further south, a cyclist sets out on the road to adventure.

107

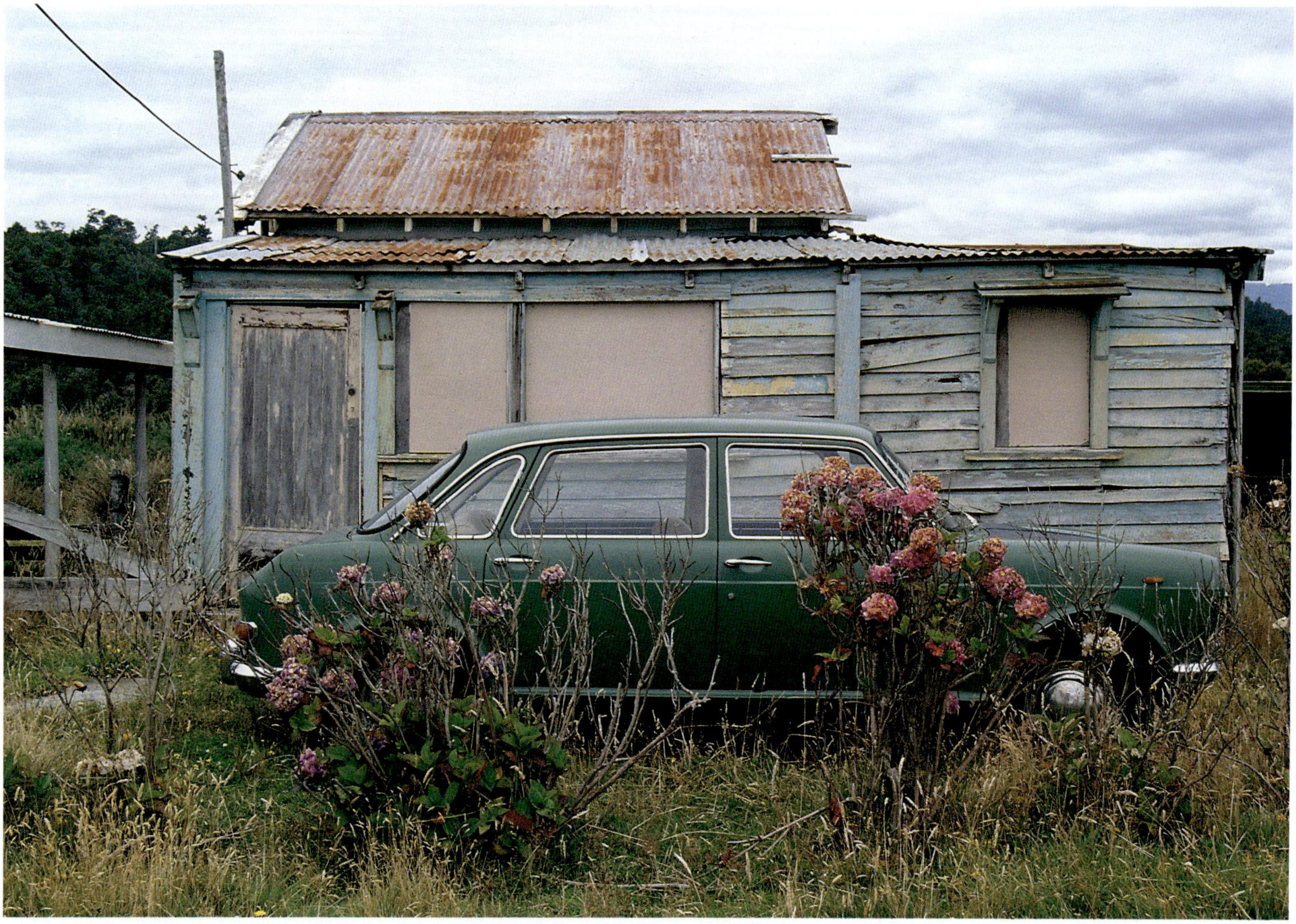

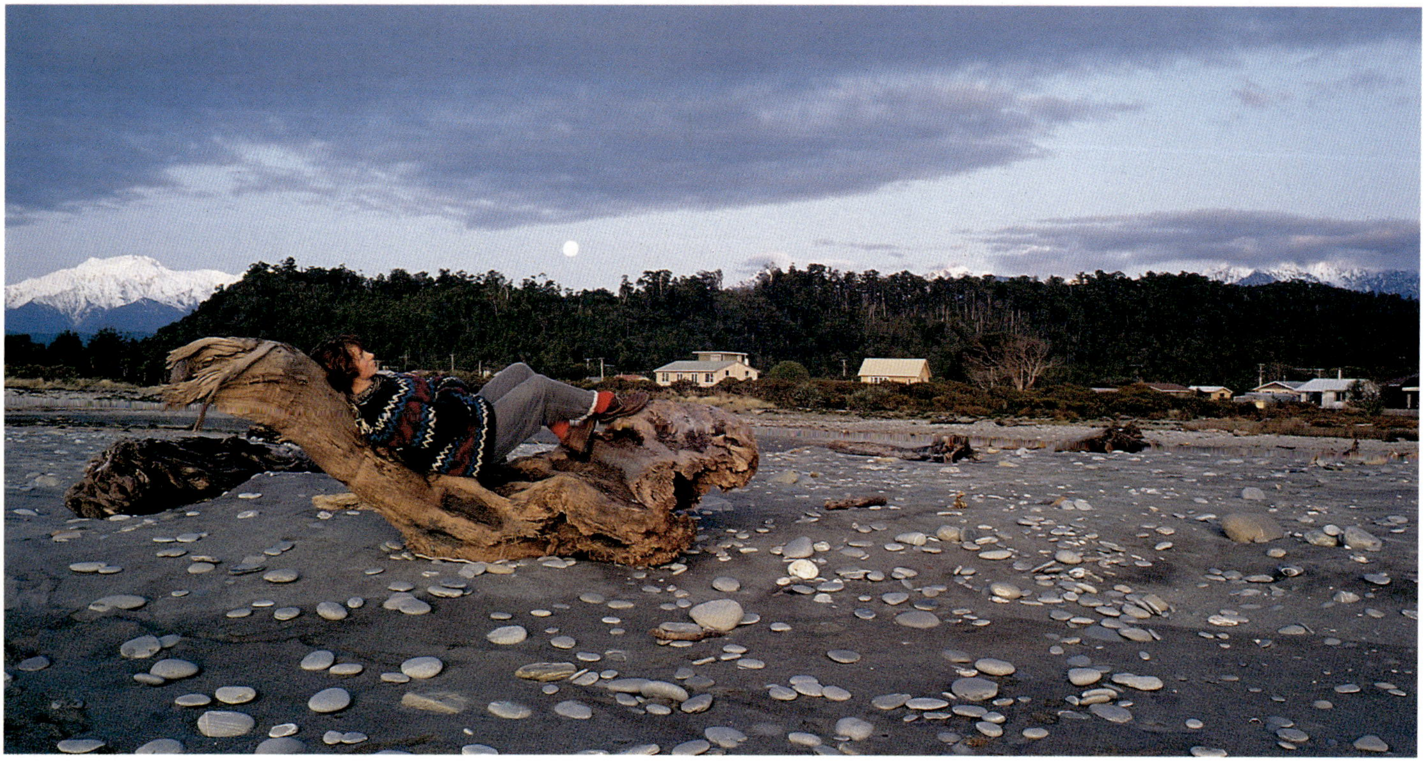

During the latter part of the nineteenth century Okarito was alive with pubs, dance halls, casinos, banks and stores, as miners flocked to join the search for gold on the Coast. Today it is a quieter place, sought for its detachment from the world, and the allure of its whitebait.

A canoeist shares the peace of Okarito Lagoon with a rare white heron, or kotuku. The only breeding ground of the kotuku is on the banks of the nearby Waitangiroto Stream.

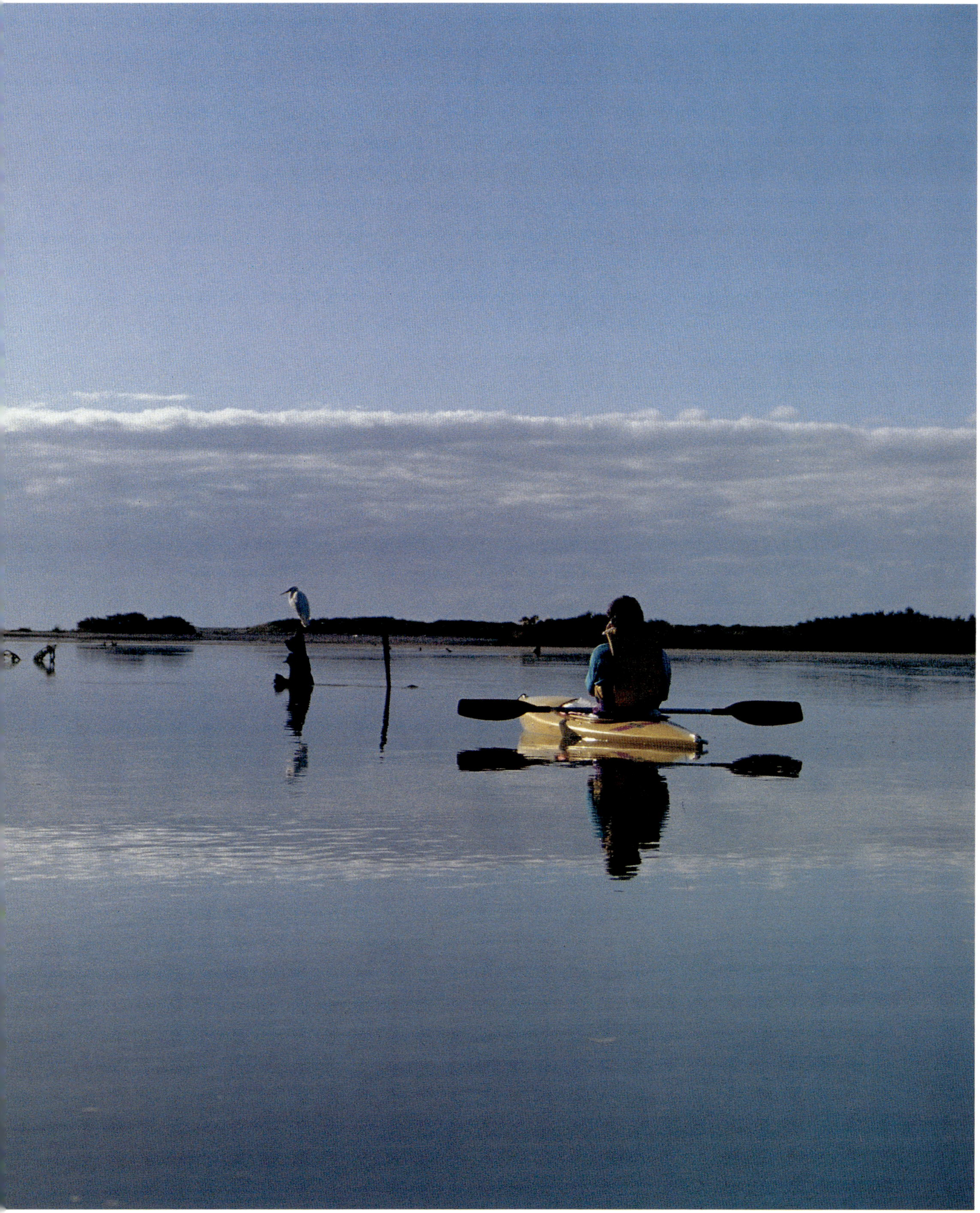

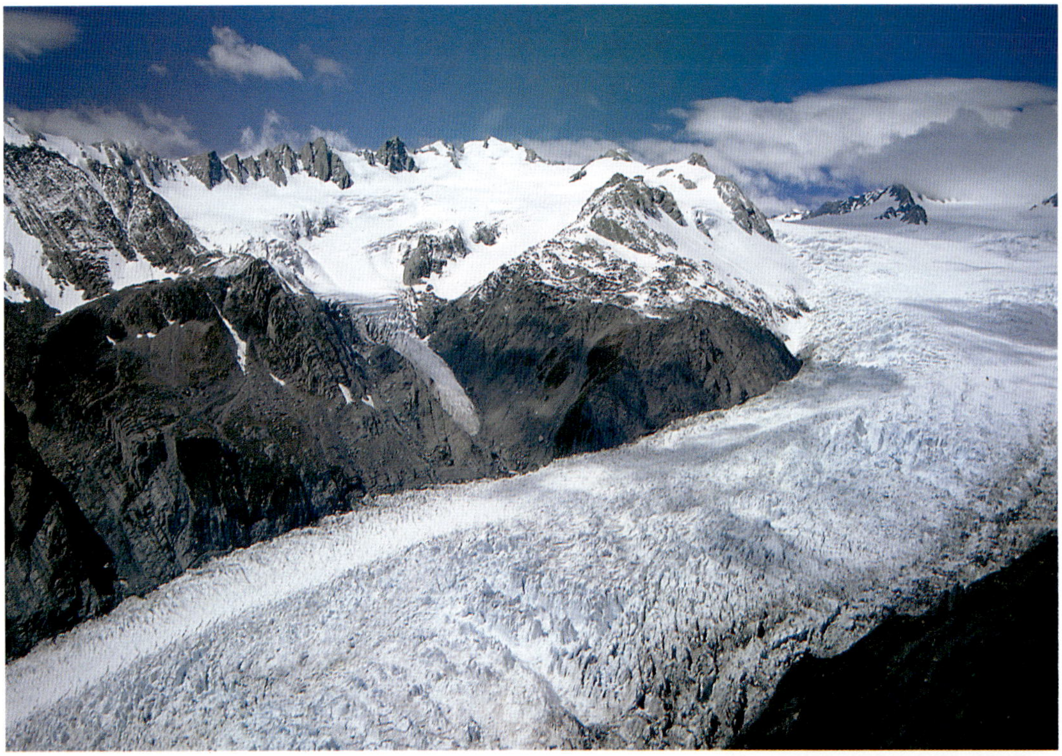

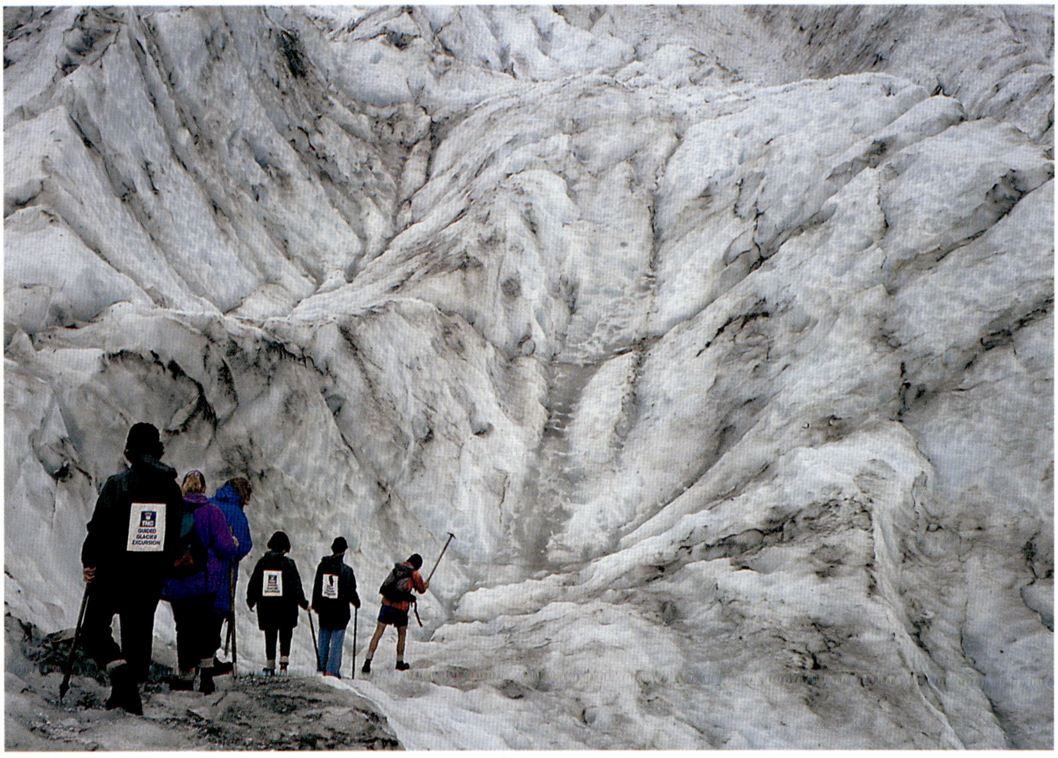

Guided walking tours take visitors right on to the magnificent Fox and Franz Josef Glaciers. At close quarters these shining rivers of ice ripple with blue and green colours and reveal jumbled blocks of ice.

Gillespies Beach is part of a rocky coast that was once part of the gold rushes, and the allure of the precious metal still calls back resolute goldpanners.

The West Coast combines superb natural beauty with an immense diversity of flora — some of the species in Westland National Park date back over 160 million years.

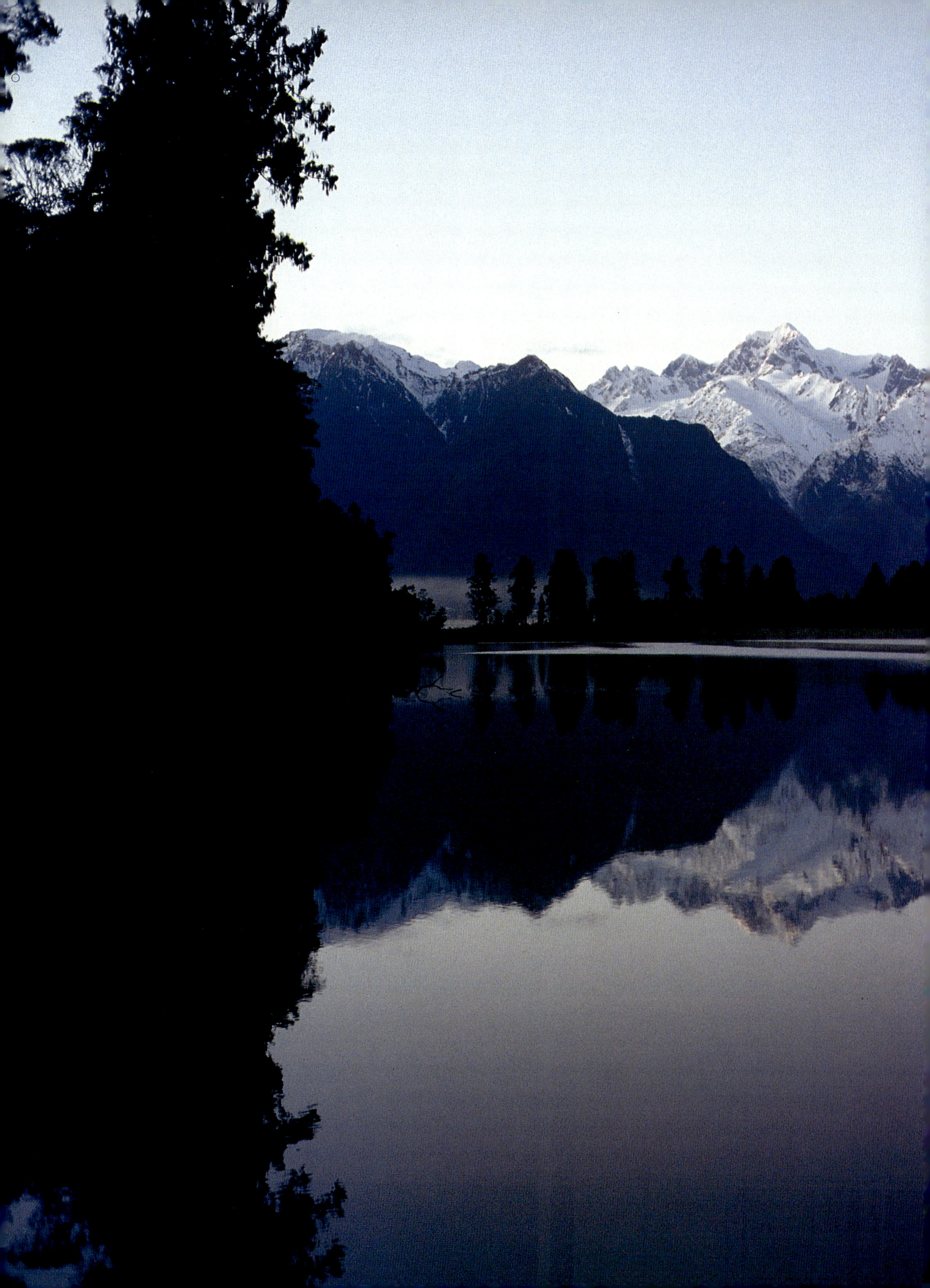

The perfect reflections of Westland's
Lake Matheson in early morning light.

The West Coast is renowned for its extraordinary weather and skyscapes. Cloud swirls over Mt Tasman (below), and a rainbow emerges after a shower (right).

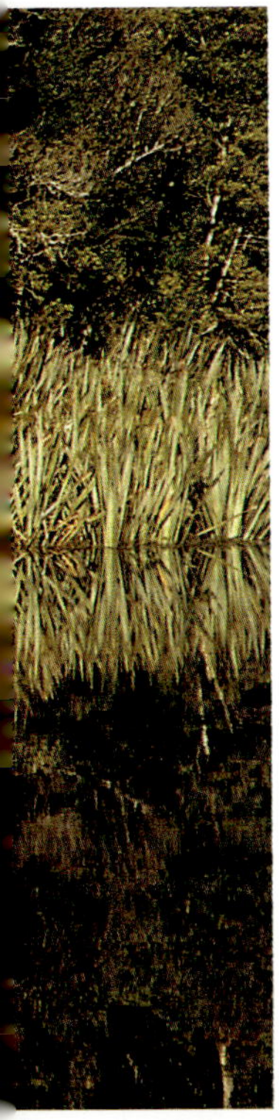

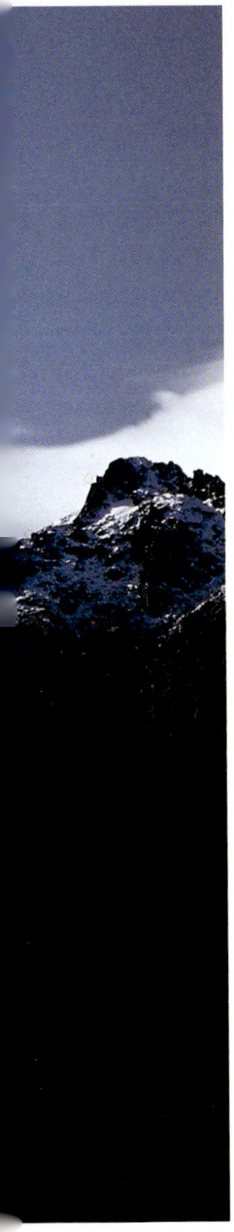

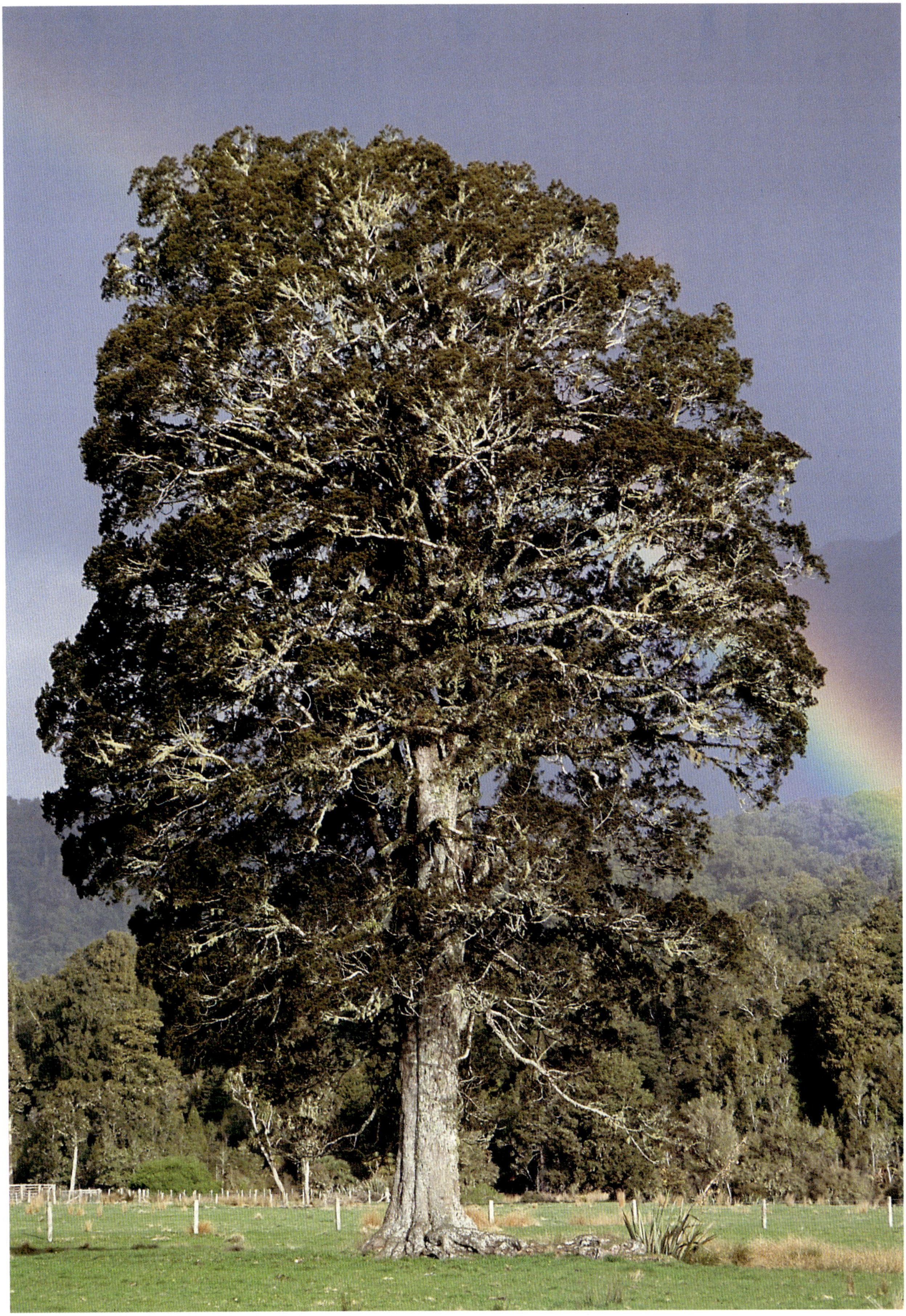

Winter landscape near Lindis Pass.

Dunedin and Otago

Otago is a place of mountains, lakes and glaciers. Most striking are The Remarkables, near Queenstown, but equally lovely are the mountains around Lakes Hawea, Wanaka and Wakatipu, where glaciers ground the hills into rounded shapes before the time of man. Then there is the Clutha, a river of immense strength, storming through steep gorges to the sea.

Queenstown is New Zealand's best-known mountain resort. An area of unsurpassable beauty, it is also a centre for adventure activities — jetboating, rafting, tramping, heliskiing or, for those who don't mind being tied by the ankles, the ultimate thrill — bungy jumping.

The earliest Europeans in Otago were whalers. As with Christchurch, however, settlers soon realised the potential of the alluvial plains, and in 1848 the ships *John Wickliffe* and *Philip Laing*, with three hundred settlers aboard, arrived in Otago Harbour. Primarily Presbyterian, the Scottish founders established Dunedin on the fortunes of great sheep stations. The discovery of gold boosted the city's coffers and, by 1871, one in every four settlers in New Zealand was to be found in Otago. By the 1880s Dunedin was the country's largest, most industrialised and pre-eminent commercial city. Although this is not the situation today, Dunedin still exerts considerable influence nationally.

Dunedin has the reputation of being the Edinburgh of the South, the result of its Scottish heritage. Constructed of grey stone, it is a handsome city, with many buildings that are perfect Victorian artefacts. Everywhere there are church spires topping churches of austere Gothic grandeur. The Municipal Chambers display a frontage in the Italian style, while the architecture of the law courts, the railway station and the university attest to a Victorian exuberance muted by a sense of respectability.

Throughout Otago there are still signs of a prosperity based on whaling, sheep rearing and gold. Otago's greatest treasure, though, is its unique landscape.

Lake Wanaka (above and centre left) and Lake Hawea (bottom left) are water-filled glaciated valleys, the result of glacier action that has smoothed and rounded the landscape below the surrounding peaks.

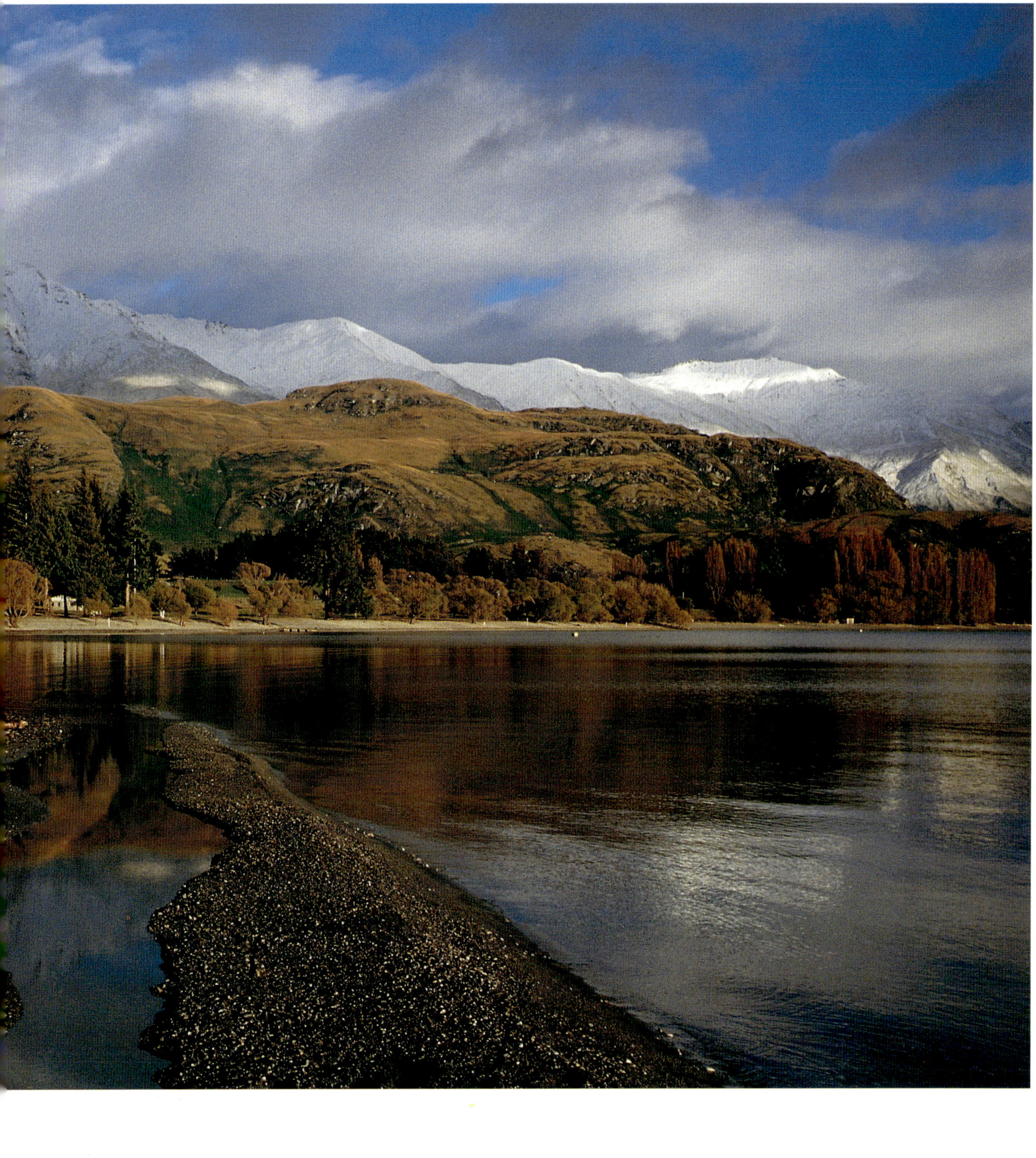

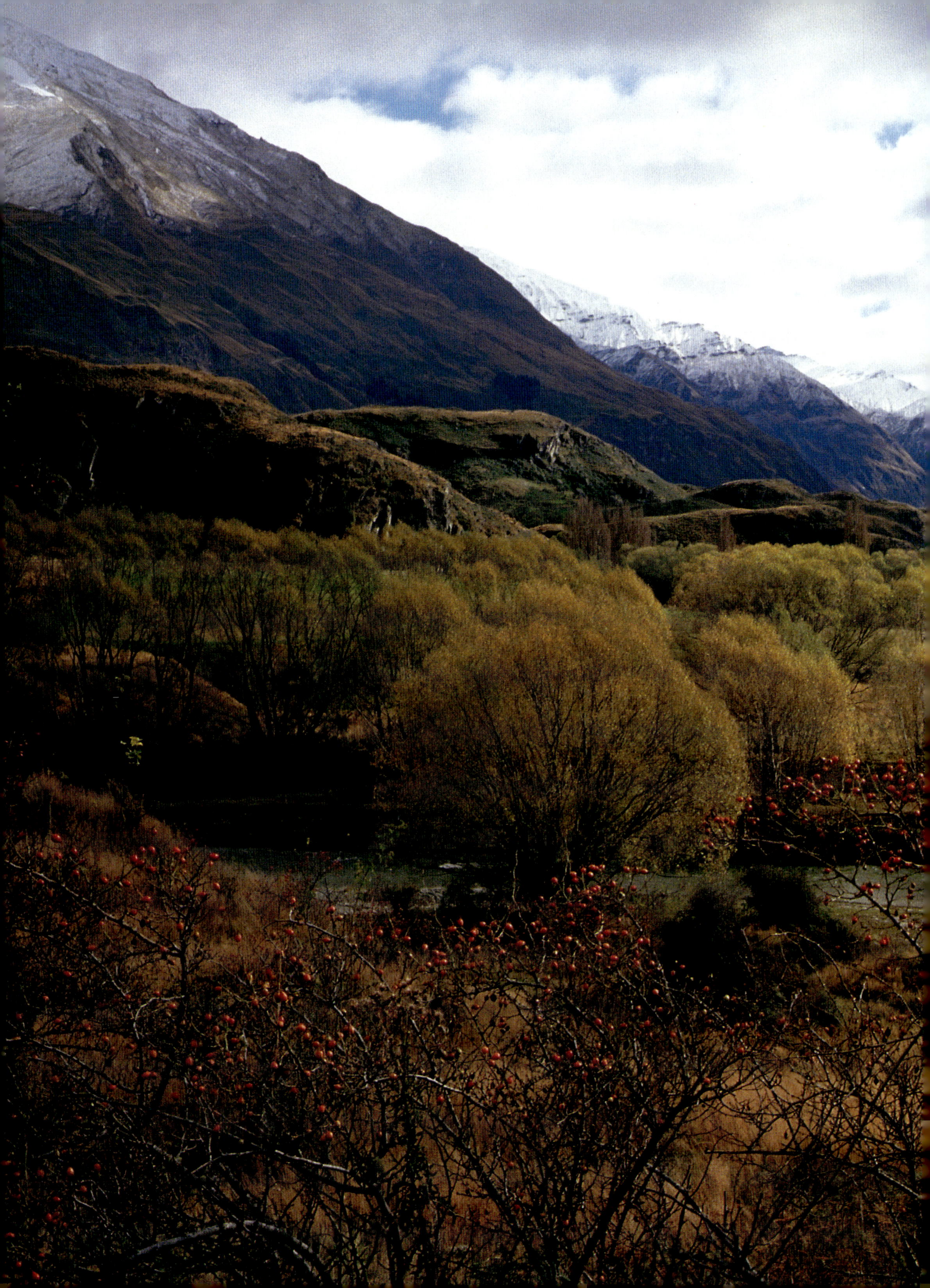

Rosehips and willows grace the
Matukituki river valley.

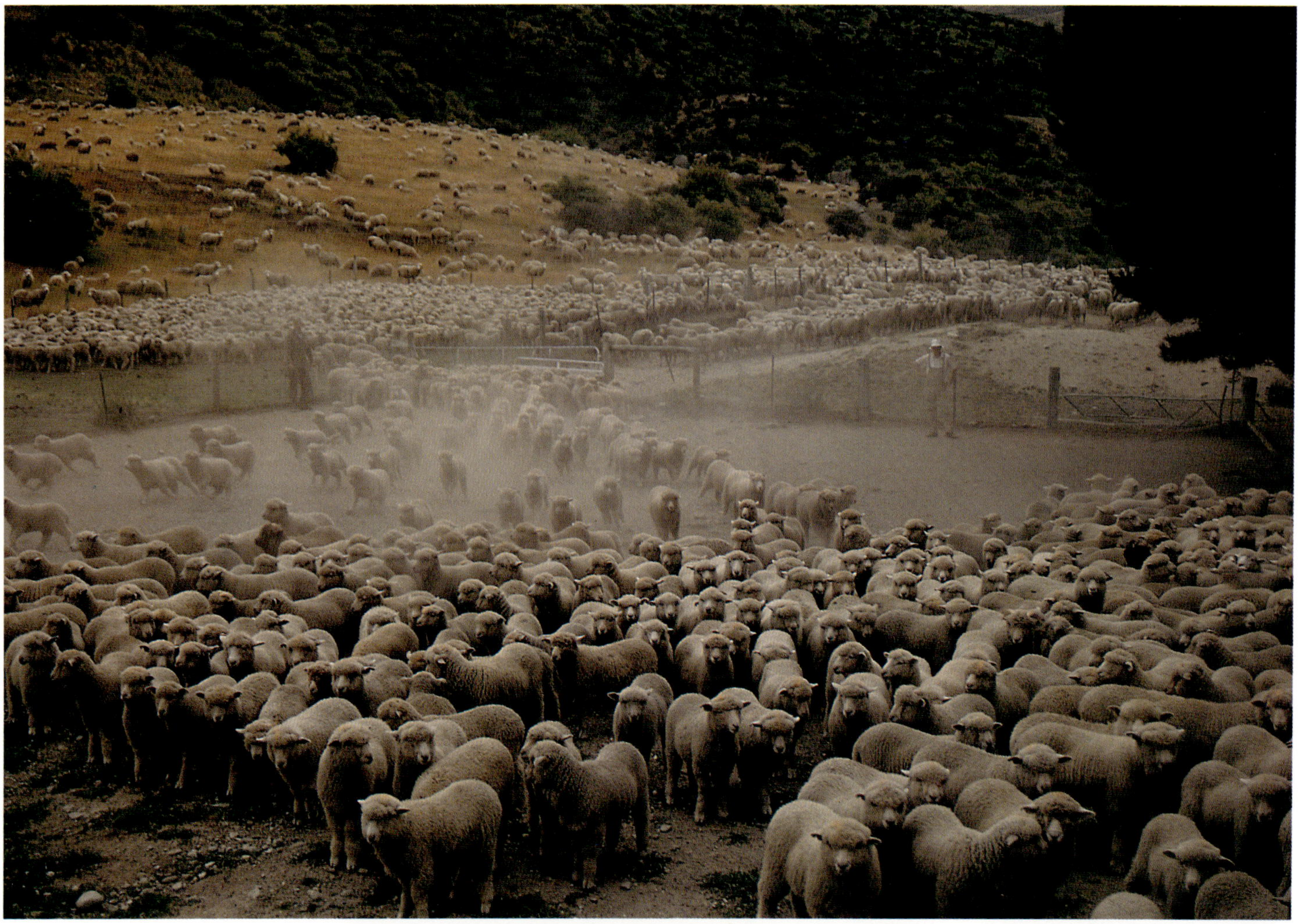

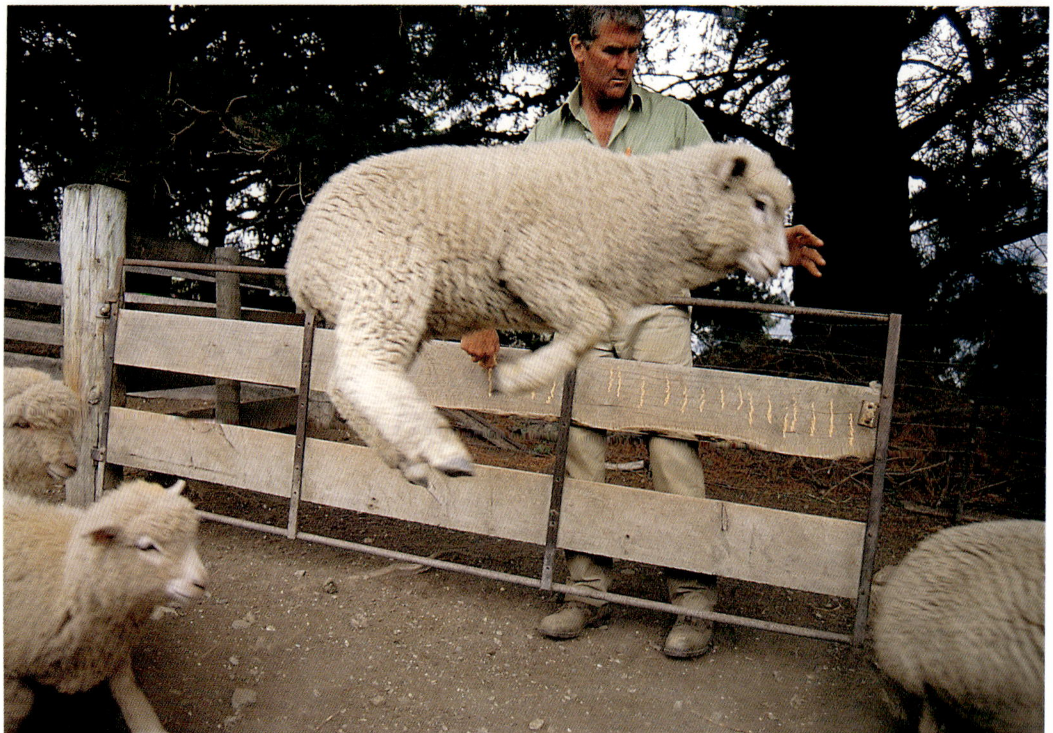

Mustering time at Loch Linnhe Station, near Queenstown. Meanwhile, on the banks of Lake Wakatipu, sheep briefly take precedence on the road.

Queenstown is the home of adventure, with bungy jumping and jet boating two of its major attractions.

If a jump from the historic Kawarau Bridge doesn't appeal, you can take a gondola ride up to Bobs Peak, high above Queenstown.

129

130

TSS *Earnslaw* is the last of four steamers that plied Lake Wakatipu during the height of the gold rush days. Queenstown nestles on the edge of the lake.

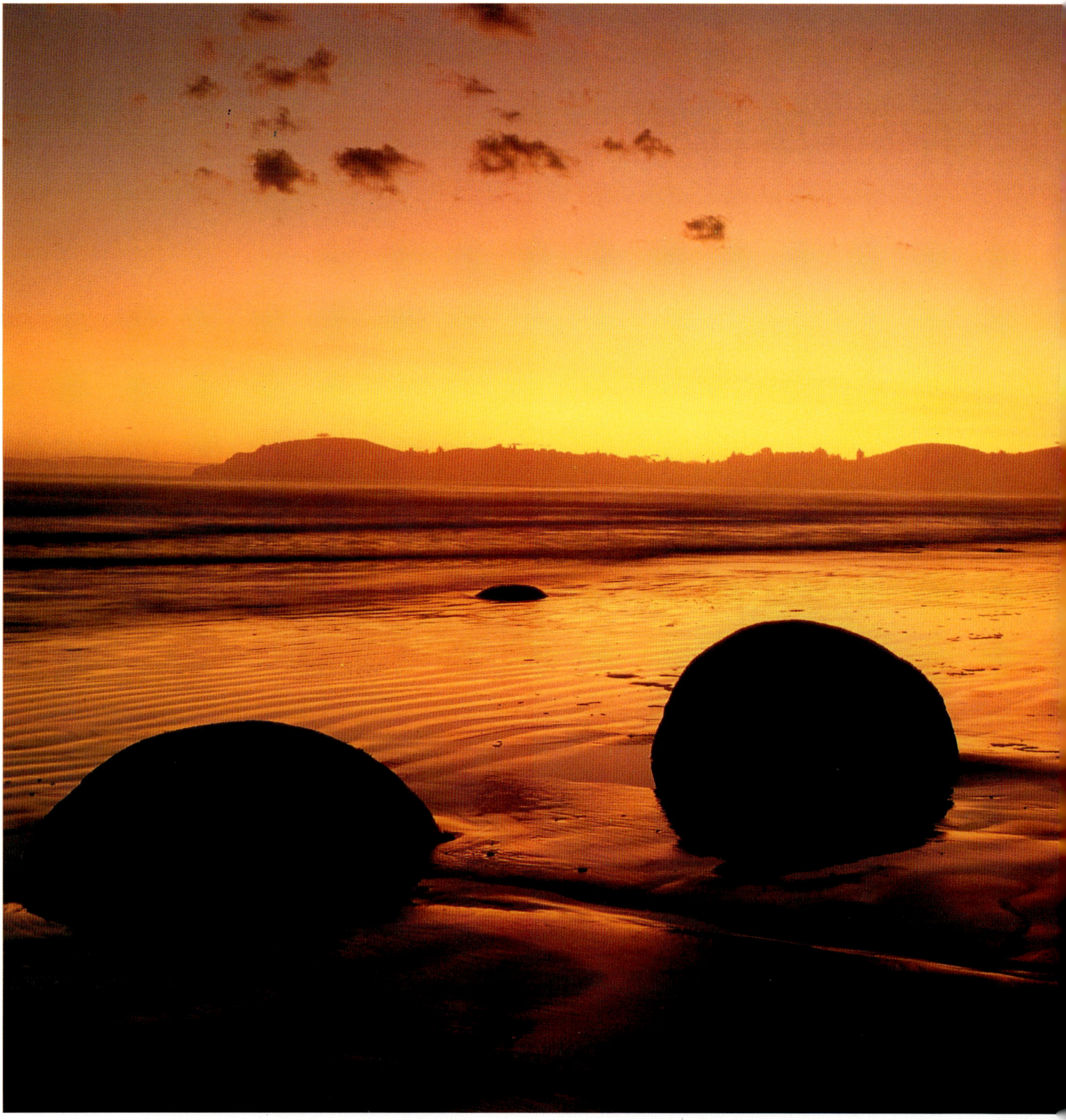

A sea lion, glistening sovereign of the seashore, roars at Moeraki Peninsula. The Moeraki coastline is steeped in Maori history, and the famed Moeraki boulders, each weighing several tonnes, are said to be the petrified food baskets of an early canoe which was wrecked on the offshore reef.

134

Taiaroa Head is the home of a famous Royal Albatross colony. Also on the Otago Peninsula is the imposing Otakou Marae. A scenic rail journey in this part of New Zealand must take in the craggy Taieri Gorge.

The University of Otago was the first university in New Zealand. The old part of the building was begun in 1870.

Larnach's Castle, built in 1871 by a wealthy banker who later became a Member of Parliament, is notable for its impressive ballroom, ornate ceilings and Italian marble fireplaces.

Dunedin Railway Station, built in 1907, is embellished with an impressive tower, magnificent mosaic floor, and stained glass windows with a distinctly 'railways' theme.

Olveston is an Edwardian residence that conjures up the elegance of a bygone era, beautifully furnished with antiques, fine paintings and memorabilia.

Lush ferns in a remote Fiordland setting.

Murihiku: The South

The southern end of Aotearoa is known to the Maori as Murihiku, and encompasses Southland, Fiordland and Stewart Island. Southland's history is similar to that of Otago. Invercargill was settled by Scots people from Dunedin in 1856, and the Scots heritage is still noticeable in the way Southlanders speak; there is a distinct burr on their r's. The new settlers found Southland similar to the Scottish highlands, and they established sheep runs on the Southland plains.

Bluff is the harbour from which agricultural produce is sent to all parts of the globe. It is also a vigorous fishing port, with catches of deep-sea fish, crayfish and shellfish. The Bluff oyster is considered by connoisseurs to be the ultimate in oysters.

Offshore from Invercargill is Stewart Island, a special place of bush-clad hills and quiet beaches. The Maori name is Rakiura, a reference to the glowing skies and auroras which play on the southern horizon.

West of Invercargill the vista opens out to the unparalleled beauty of Fiordland National Park. Sea and the massive forces of the Ice Ages have created astounding physical configurations to the land. Every day rain, wind, cloud and sleet combine to recreate an everchanging panorama. Along the coast are the great fiords — Milford, Bligh, Caswell, Nancy, Doubtful, Dusky and Preservation Inlet. Inland are the Takitimu Mountains and the lakes Te Anau and Manapouri, and the magnificent Milford Track, a walk which has been called the finest in the world.

The superb Catlins coast has a rugged grandeur that, once experienced, is never forgotten.

Nugget Point lighthouse surveys a rocky coast. In contrast, the small church at Waikawa is serene in the sunshine.

141

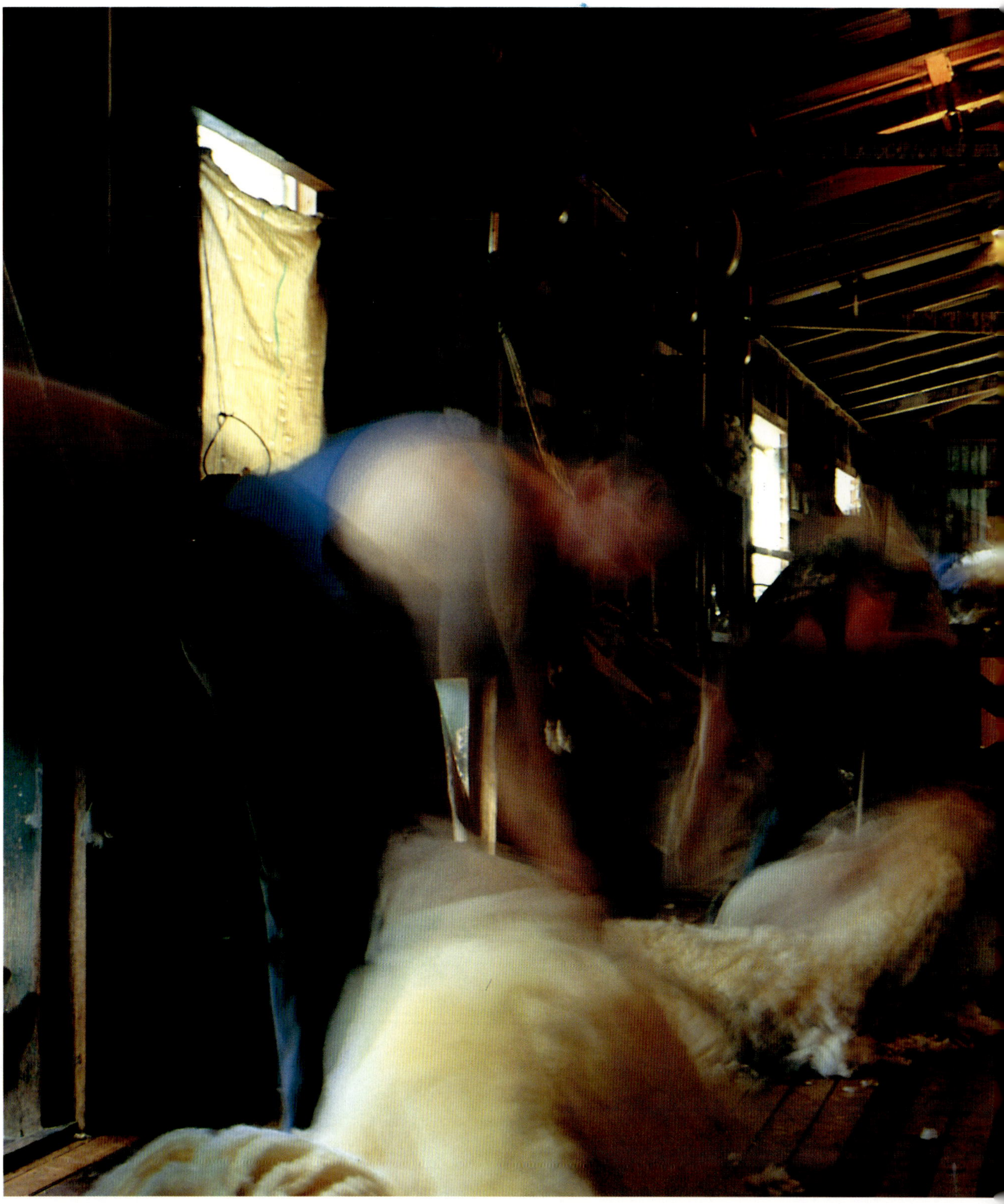

Sheep shearing is a fast and furious business — definitely not for the fainthearted.

A field of wild flowers on the road to Milford Sound. Milford is dominated by Mitre Peak, rising steeply from the deep waters of the fiord.

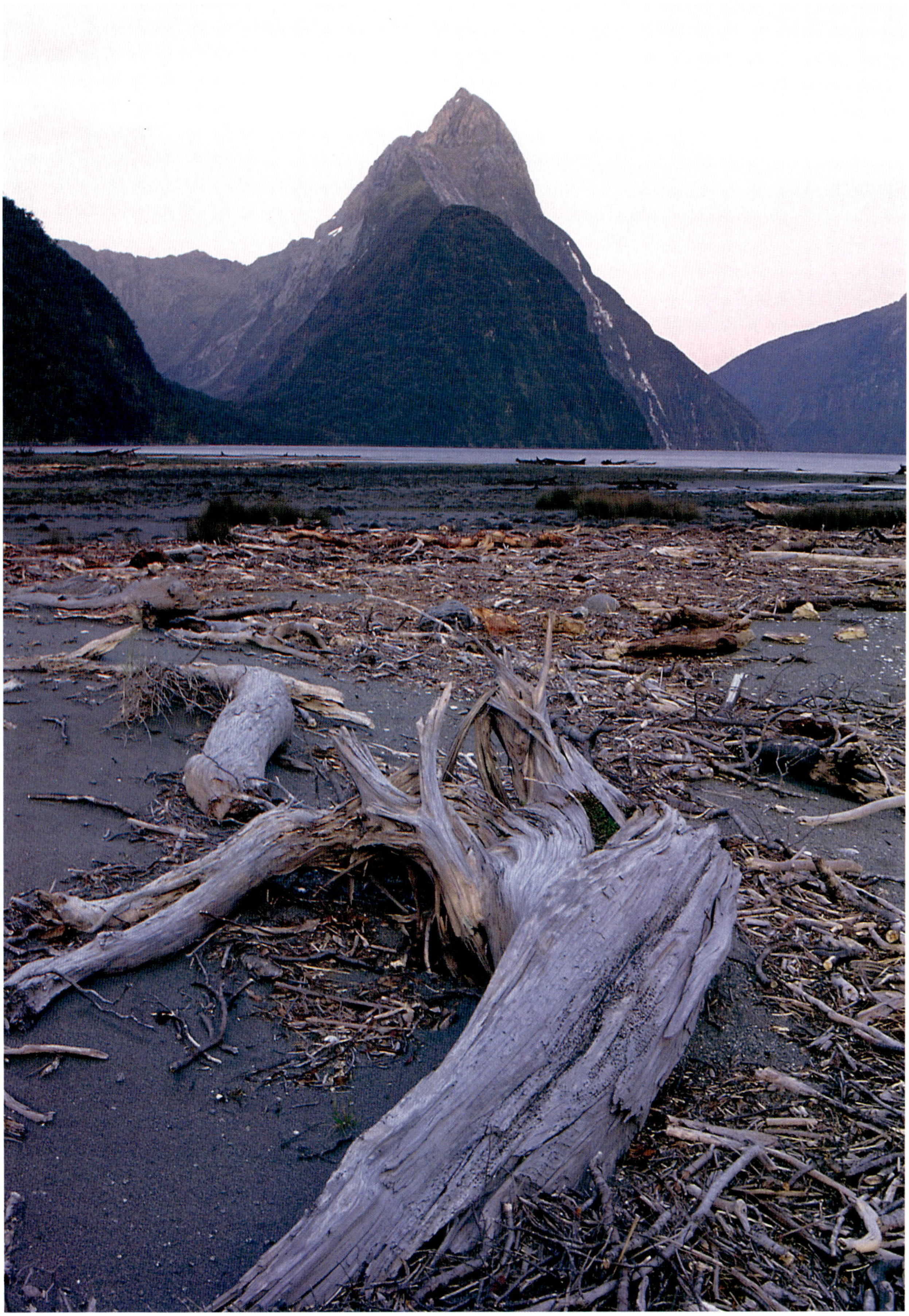

Trampers experience all types of conditions on the 54-kilometre Milford Track, often described as 'the finest walk in the world'. The magnificent Bowen Falls drop down into Milford Sound.

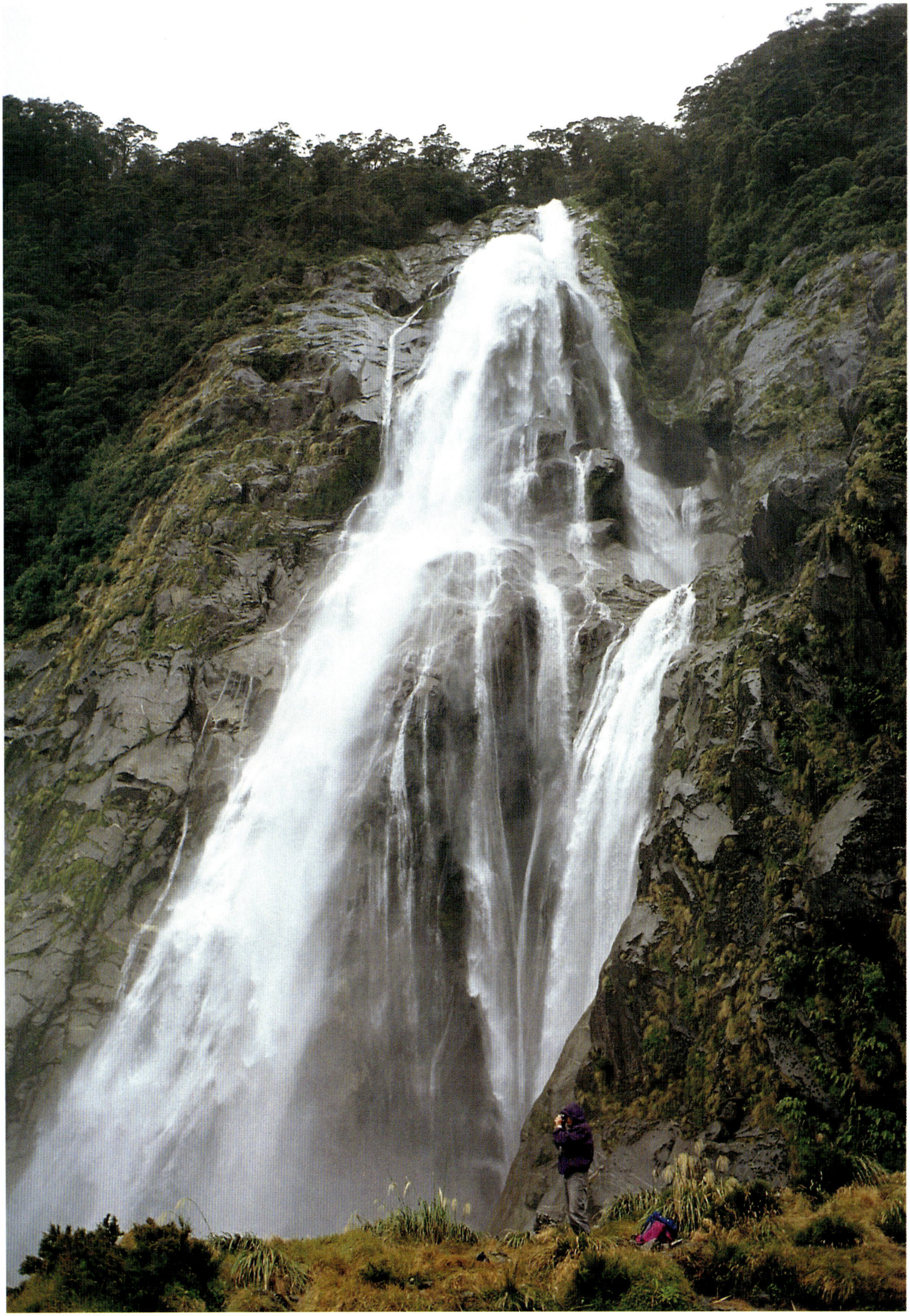

Dawn at Cascade Cove, Dusky Sound,
and half-light at Acheron Passage.

Doubtful Sound, named Doubtfull Harbour by Captain Cook in 1770, is one of the most haunting of the numerous southern fiords. Nearby, morning mist hovers over the rainforest.

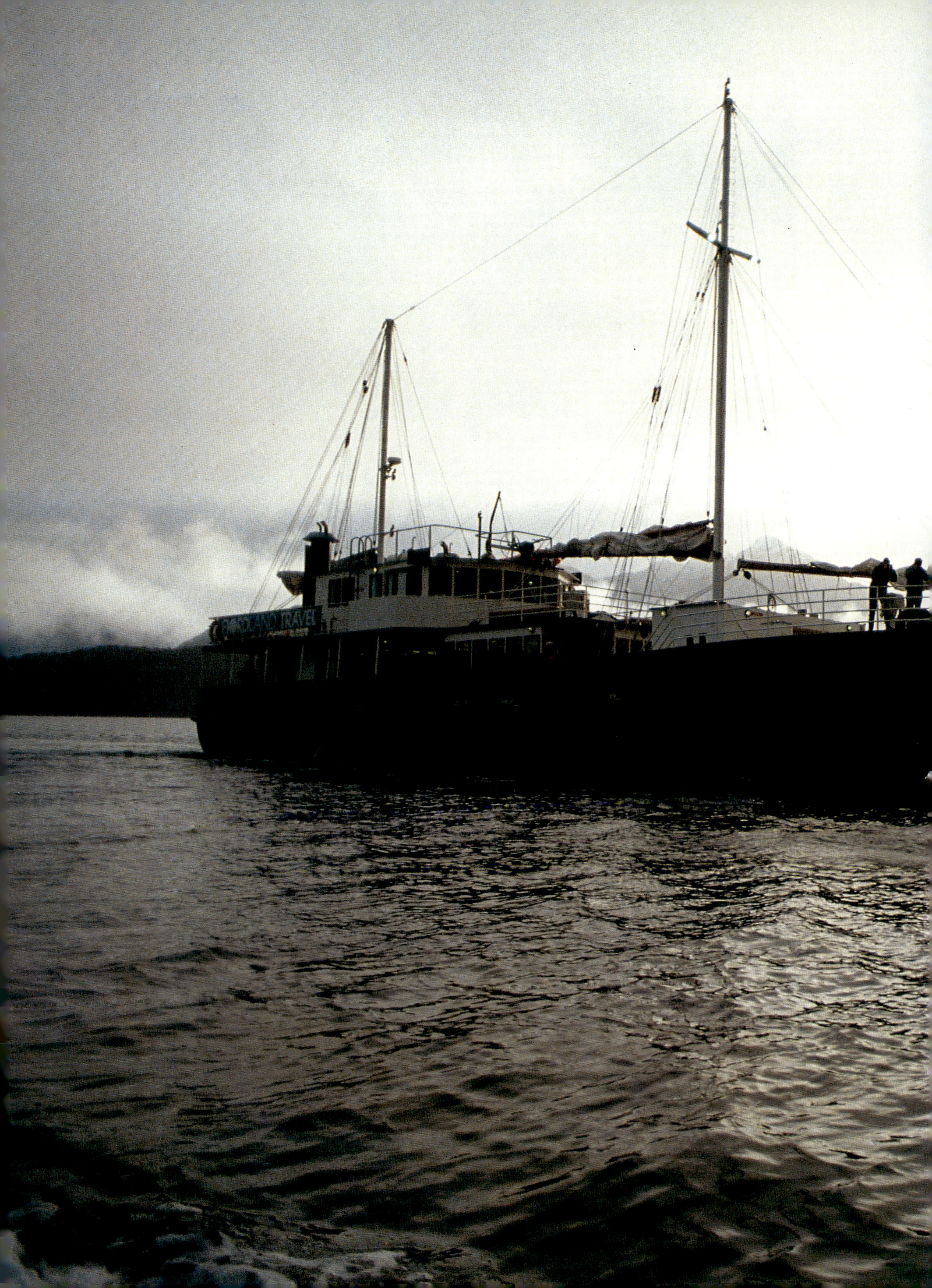
TRAVEL

A playful dolphin leaps before the Milford Wanderer, scouting across the mist-shrouded waters of Dusky Sound.

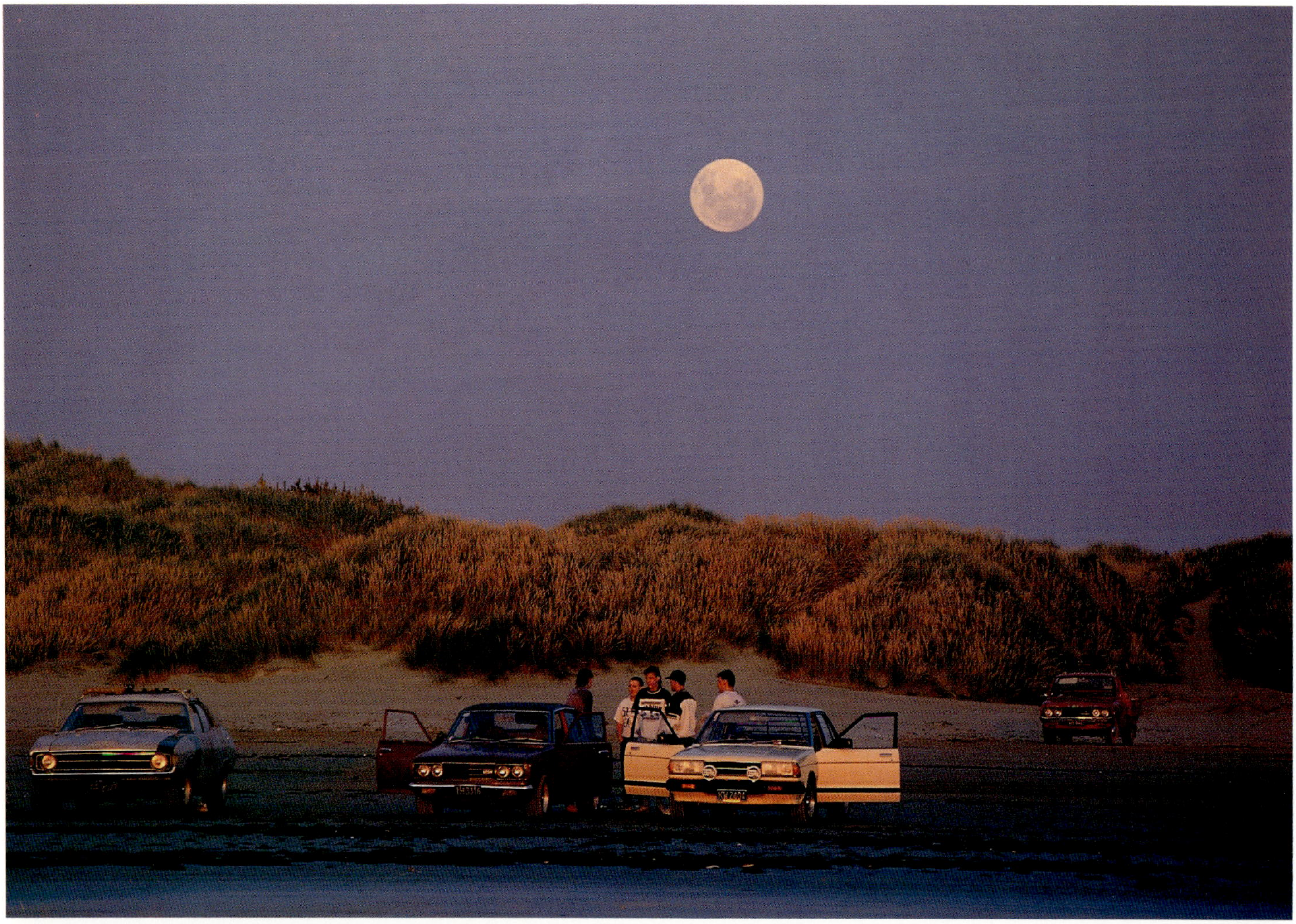

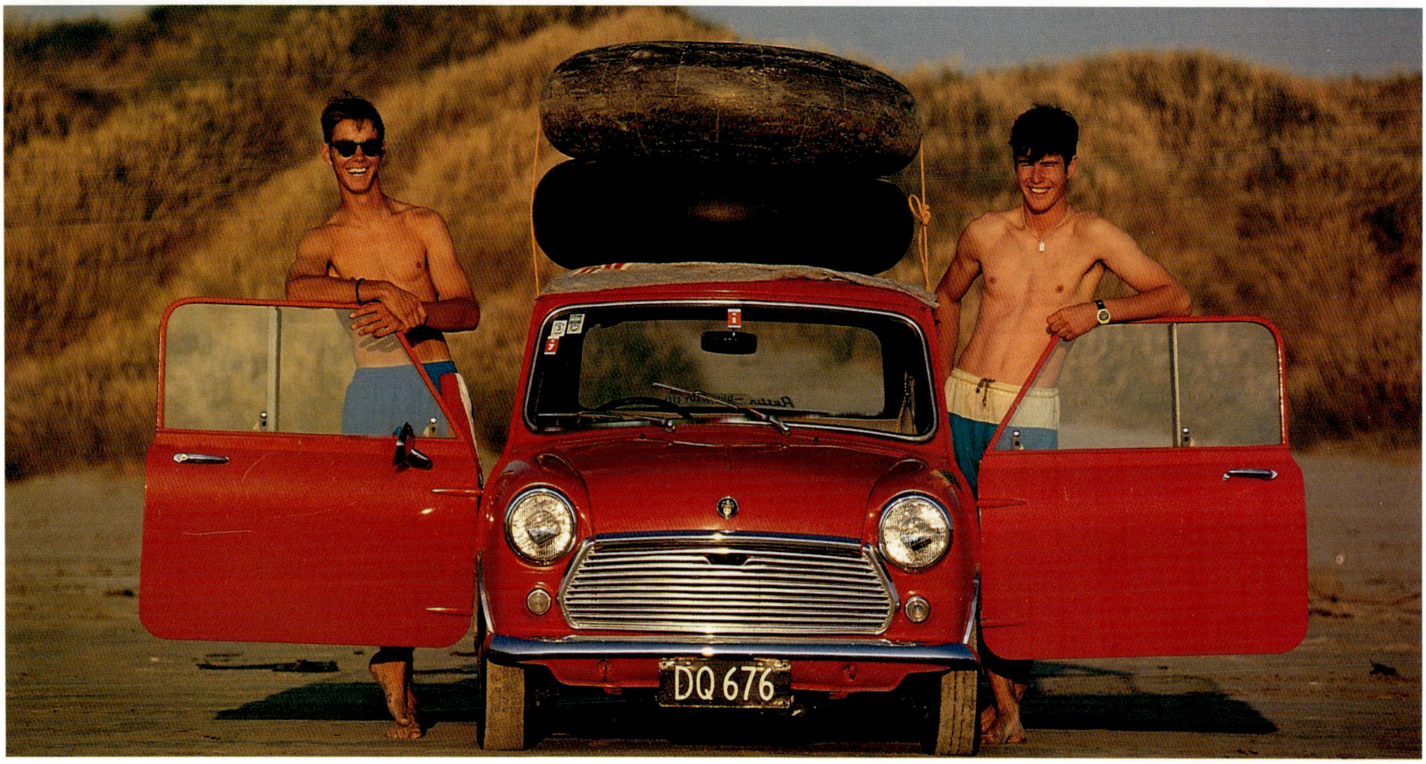
DQ 676

No matter where you are, you will always find surfers chasing the waves, even here at Oreti Beach, among the most southern waves of the world.

The tuatara, often called New Zealand's living dinosaur. Southland Museum in Invercargill has the country's most successful breeding programme.

In Bluff, at the very bottom of the South Island, Fred and Myrtle Flutey have turned their house into a showcase for the paua shell.

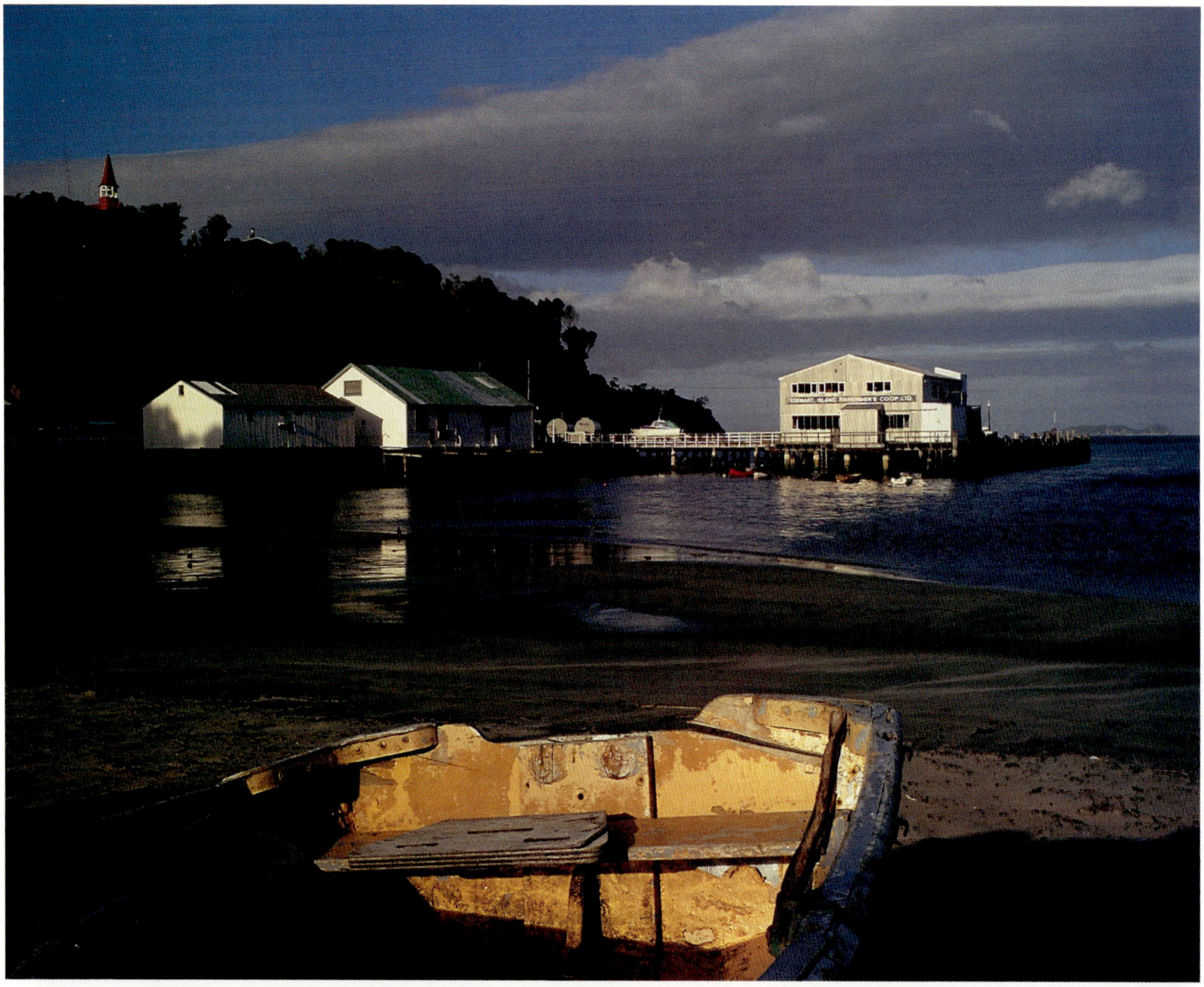
STEWART ISLAND FISHERMEN'S CO-OP LTD

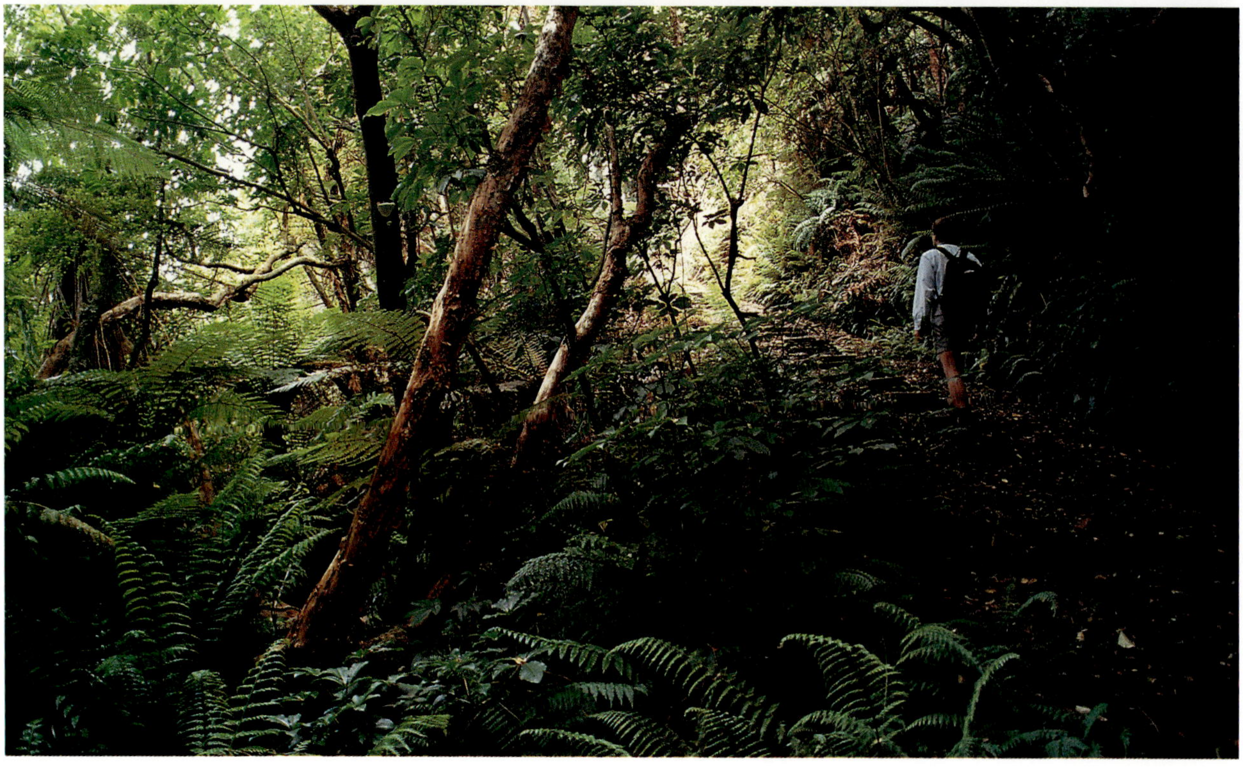

Stewart Island is a special place. Remote and sparsely populated, it has great appeal to trampers and others seeking peace and tranquillity. It also supports a vigorous fishing industry.

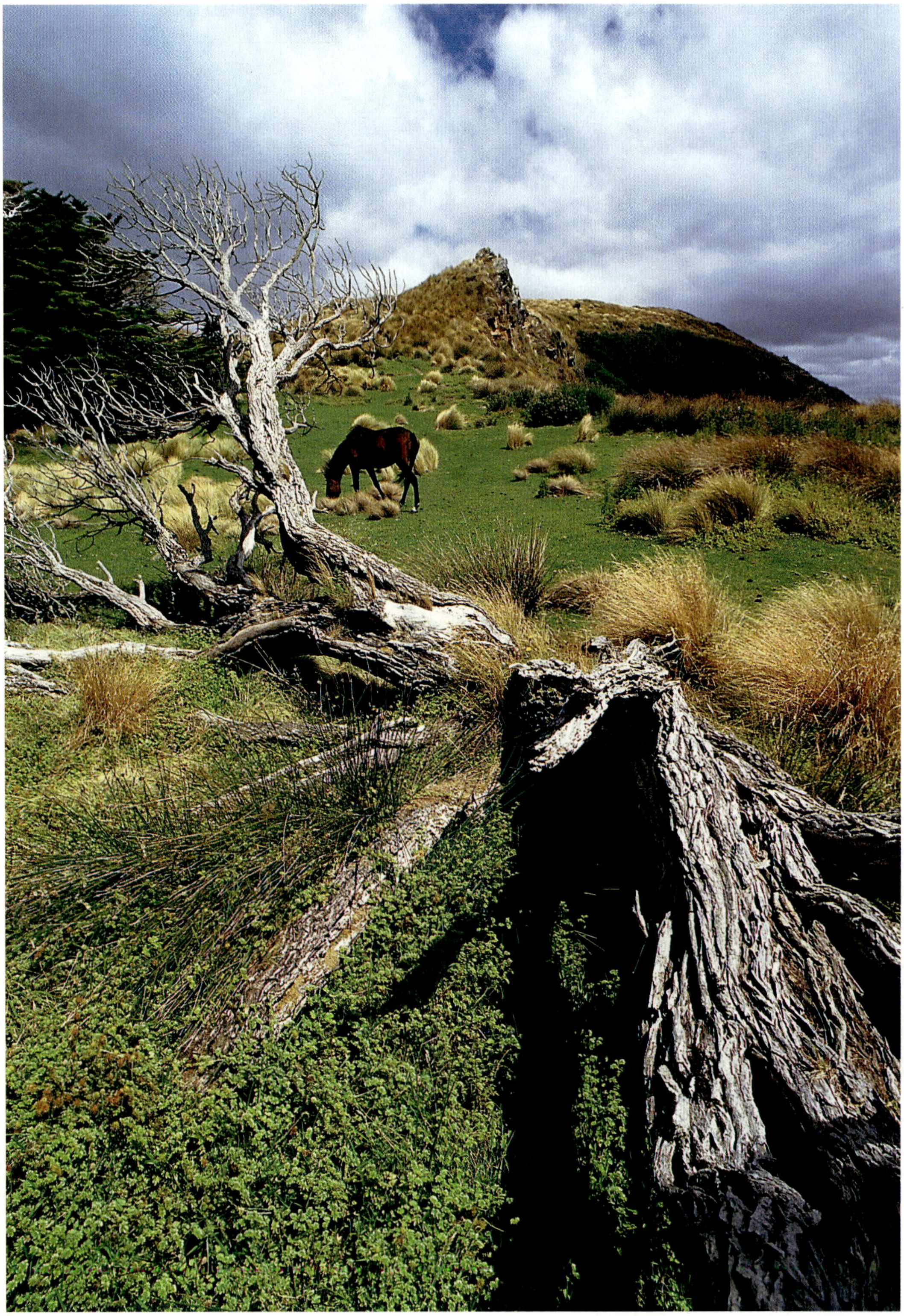

Stewart Island's Maori name is Rakiura, aptly translated as 'island of glowing skies'.

Acknowledgements

Thank you to the many New Zealanders who welcomed me to Aotearoa and made me feel at home.

And thank you, friends and fellow travellers, for the inspiration and the best of times. You know who you are.

— H.L.

Thanks to Montana Wines Ltd and Air New Zealand for travel assistance in the South Island, and to Holger Leue, Ian Watt, Susan Brierley, Chris Lipscombe and Alison Jacobs.

— W.I.